Ending violence against women
From words to action

Study of the Secretary-General

UNITED NATIONS

NOTE

The designations employed and the presentation of the material in this publication do not imply the expression of any opinion whatsoever on the part of the Secretariat of the United Nations concerning the legal status of any country, territory, city or area or of its authorities, or concerning the delimitation of its frontiers or boundaries. The term "country" as used in the text of this publication also refers, as appropriate, to territories or areas.

Symbols of United Nations documents are composed of capital letters combined with figures.

This publication has been issued without formal editing.

UNITED NATIONS PUBLICATION

Sales No. E.06.IV.8

ISBN-10: 92-1-112703-3

ISBN-13: 978-92-1-112703-4

EXECUTIVE SUMMARY

Violence against women is a form of discrimination and a violation of human rights. It causes untold misery, cutting short lives and leaving countless women living in pain and fear in every country in the world. It harms families across the generations, impoverishes communities and reinforces other forms of violence throughout societies. Violence against women stops them from fulfilling their potential, restricts economic growth and undermines development. The scope and extent of violence against women are a reflection of the degree and persistence of discrimination that women continue to face. It can only be eliminated, therefore, by addressing discrimination, promoting women's equality and empowerment, and ensuring that women's human rights are fulfilled.

All of humanity would benefit from an end to this violence, and there has been considerable progress in creating the international framework for achieving this. However, new forms of violence have emerged and, in some countries, advances towards equality and freedom from violence previously made by women have been eroded or are under threat. The continued prevalence of violence against women is testimony to the fact that States have yet to tackle it with the necessary political commitment, visibility and resources.

Violence against women is neither unchanging nor inevitable and could be radically reduced, and eventually eliminated, with the necessary political will and resources. This study identifies ways to close the gap between States' obligations under international norms, standards and policies and their inadequate and inconsistent implementation at the national level. It calls for efforts to eradicate violence against women to become a higher priority at the local, national and international level.

Overview

Violence against women was drawn out of the private domain into public attention and the arena of State accountability largely because of the grass-roots work of women's organizations and movements around the world. This work drew attention to the fact that violence against women is not the result of random, individual acts of misconduct, but rather is deeply rooted in structural relationships of inequality between women and men. The interaction between women's advocacy and United Nations initiatives has been a driving factor in establishing violence against women as a human rights issue on the international agenda.

There has been significant progress in elaborating and agreeing on international standards and norms. International and regional legal and policy instruments have clarified the obligations on States to prevent, eradicate and punish violence against women. However, States around the world are failing to meet the requirements of the international legal and policy framework.

Causes and risk factors

The roots of violence against women lie in historically unequal power relations between men and women and pervasive discrimination against women in both the public and private spheres. Patriarchal disparities of power, discriminatory cultural norms and economic inequalities serve to deny women's human rights and perpetuate violence. Violence against women is one of the key means through which male control over women's agency and sexuality is maintained.

Within the broad context of women's subordination, specific causal factors for violence include the use of violence to resolve conflicts, doctrines of privacy and State inaction. Individual or family behaviour patterns, including histories of abuse, have also been correlated with an increased risk of violence.

Violence against women is not confined to a specific culture, region or country, or to particular groups of women within a society. The different manifestations of such violence and women's personal experiences are, however, shaped by factors such as ethnicity, class, age, sexual orientation, disability, nationality and religion.

Forms and consequences

There are many different forms of violence against women—physical, sexual, psychological and economic. Some increase in importance while others diminish as societies undergo demographic changes, economic restructuring and social and cultural shifts. For example, new technologies may generate new forms of violence, such as internet or mobile telephone stalking. Some forms, such as international trafficking and violence against migrant workers, cross national boundaries.

Women are subjected to violence in a wide range of settings, including the family, the community, state custody, and armed conflict and its aftermath. Violence constitutes a continuum across the lifespan of women, from before birth to old age. It cuts across both the public and the private spheres.

The most common form of violence experienced by women globally is intimate partner violence, sometimes leading to death. Also widespread are harmful traditional practices, including early and forced marriage and female genital mutilation/cutting. Within the community setting, femicide (gender-based murder of women), sexual violence, sexual harassment and trafficking in women are receiving increasing attention. Violence perpetrated by the State, through its agents, through omission, or through public policy, spans physical, sexual and psychological violence. It can constitute torture. The high incidence of violence against women in armed conflict, particularly sexual violence including rape, has become progressively clearer.

Violence against women has far-reaching consequences for women, their children, and society as a whole. Women who experience violence suffer a range of health problems, and their ability to earn a living and to participate in public life is diminished. Their children are significantly more at risk of health problems, poor school performance and behavioural disturbances.

Violence against women impoverishes women, their families, communities and nations. It lowers economic production, drains resources from public services and employers, and reduces human capital formation. While even the most comprehensive surveys to date underestimate the costs, they all show that the failure to address violence against women has serious economic consequences.

The knowledge base

There is compelling evidence that violence against women is severe and pervasive throughout the world: in 71 countries at least one survey on violence against women has been conducted. However, there is still an urgent need to strengthen the knowledge base to inform policy and strategy development.

Many countries lack reliable data and much of the existing information cannot be meaningfully compared. Few countries carry out regular data collection, which would allow changes over time to be measured. Information is urgently needed on how various forms of violence affect different groups of women—this requires data that has been disaggregated according to factors such as age and ethnicity. Little information is available to assess the measures taken to combat violence against women and to evaluate their impact. Ensuring adequate data collection is part of every State's obligation to address violence against women, but inadequate data does not diminish State responsibility for preventing and eliminating violence against women.

A set of international indicators on violence against women should be established, based on widely available and credible data collected at the national level, using comparable methods to define and measure violence.

State responsibility

States have concrete and clear obligations to address violence against women, whether committed by state agents or by non-state actors. States are accountable to women themselves, to all their citizens and to the international community. States have a duty to prevent acts of violence against women; to investigate such acts when they occur and prosecute and punish perpetrators; and to provide redress and relief to the victims.

While differing circumstances and constraints require different types of action to be taken by the State, they do not excuse State inaction. Yet States worldwide are failing to implement in full the international standards on violence against women.

When the State fails to hold the perpetrators of violence accountable, this not only encourages further abuses, it also gives the message that male violence against women is acceptable or normal. The result of such impunity is not only denial of justice to the individual victims/survivors, but also reinforcement of prevailing inequalities that affect other women and girls as well.

Promising practices

Many States have developed good or promising practices to prevent or respond to violence against women. State strategies to address violence should promote women's agency and be based on women's experiences and involvement, and on partnerships with non-governmental organizations (NGOs) and other civil society actors. Women's NGOs in many countries have engaged in innovative projects and programmes, sometimes in collaboration with the State.

Generic aspects of good or promising practices can be extracted from a variety of experiences around the world. Common principles include: clear policies and laws; strong enforcement mechanisms; motivated and well-trained personnel; the involvement of multiple sectors; and close collaboration with local women's groups, civil society organizations, academics and professionals.

Many governments use national plans of action—which include legal measures, service provision and prevention strategies—to address violence against women. The most effective include consultation with women's groups and other civil society organizations, clear time lines and benchmarks, transparent mechanisms for monitoring implementation, indicators of impact and evaluation, predictable and adequate funding streams, and integration of measures to tackle violence against women in programmes in a variety of sectors.

The way forward: a question of priorities

Violence against women is complex and diverse in its manifestations. Its elimination requires a comprehensive and systematic response by States, the United Nations, and all stakeholders. Local communities also have a responsibility for addressing violence against women and they should be assisted in doing so. Men have a role, especially in preventing violence, and this role needs to be further explored and strengthened.

Strong institutional mechanisms are required at national and international level to ensure action, coordination, monitoring and accountability.

■ **States should take urgent and concrete measures to secure gender equality and protect women's human rights**

Violence against women is both a cause and a consequence of discrimination against women. States have an obligation to respect, protect, promote and fulfill all human rights, including the right of women to be free from discrimination. Failure to do so results in and exacerbates violence against women. For example, if States fail to criminalize certain forms of violence against women or allow discriminatory penal laws to remain in force, then these acts may be perpetrated with impunity.

■ **The exercise of leadership is essential to end violence against women**

Leadership is critical at all levels (local, national, regional and international) and by all sectors (including politicians and government officials, opinion formers, business leaders, civil society organizations and community leaders).

■ **States must close the gaps between international standards and national laws, policies and practices**

Ending impunity and ensuring accountability for violence against women are crucial to prevent and reduce such violence. Impunity for violence against women (by both state and non-state actors) results from the failure of States to implement international standards at the national and local level. States have a responsibility to act with due diligence to prevent violence against women; to investigate such violence; to prosecute and punish perpetrators, whether they are state or non-state actors; and to provide access to redress for victims.

■ **States should build and sustain strong multisectoral strategies, coordinated nationally and locally**

Work to end violence against women requires not only a clear demonstration of political commitment but also systematic and sustained action, backed by strong, dedicated and permanent institutional mechanisms. States should build on the work done by NGOs, scale up and institutionalize it and share experiences with other countries.

■ **States should allocate adequate resources and funding to programmes to address and redress violence against women**

The social, political and economic costs of allowing this violence to continue unabated are great and call for a commensurate investment in women's security. Such an effort requires increased political will expressed through a much greater commitment of financial and human resources. Sectors such as justice, health, housing and education are critical in assisting women who survive violence to access effective legal, health and social services, as well as in enhancing prevention work.

■ **The knowledge base on all forms of violence against women should be strengthened to inform policy and strategy development**

Information that assesses and evaluates what policies and practices are most effective is particularly scarce. Governments should take responsibility for the systematic collection and publication of data, including supporting NGOs, academics or others engaged in such activities.

The United Nations system can do more to strengthen the capacity of States to collect, process and disseminate data on violence against women. As a priority, a United Nations working group should be convened to develop a set of international indicators for assessing the prevalence of violence against women and the impact of different interventions. An internationally comparable database on physical intimate partner violence could be built within seven years.

■ **The United Nations should take a stronger, better coordinated and more visible leadership role to address violence against women**

In particular, the General Assembly should consider the question of violence against women annually and the Security Council should consider establishing a dedicated monitoring mechanism within the framework of resolution 1325 on women, peace and security, to enhance its contribution to preventing and redressing violence against women. Other inter-governmental bodies should also contribute to the elimination of violence against women within the framework of their mandates.

The Special Adviser to the Secretary-General on Gender Issues and Advancement of Women should spearhead United Nations efforts, providing leadership and coordination. Greater priority should also be given in United Nations operational activities at the country level to tackling violence against women, including in humanitarian assistance and peacekeeping missions.

■ **The resources allocated throughout the United Nations system to address violence against women should be increased significantly**

States, donors and international organizations should increase significantly the financial support for work on violence against women in United Nations agencies and programmes.

Violence against women must be given greater priority at all levels—it has not yet received the priority required to enable significant change. Leadership is critical. Much can be achieved with political will, but there is also a need for considerable investment of resources and for consistent assistance, especially to the least developed countries and countries emerging from conflict. A more cohesive and strategic approach is needed from all actors, including governments, the international community and civil society.

Acknowledgements

The Secretary-General's in-depth study on violence against women, mandated by General Assembly resolution 58/185, was prepared by the Division for the Advancement of Women of the Department of Economic and Social Affairs of the United Nations Secretariat.

Expert inputs for the study were provided by two expert group meetings organized by the Division for the Advancement of Women. One meeting, on data and statistics, was organized in collaboration with the Economic Commission for Europe and the World Health Organization (WHO), with the participation of the following experts: Elizabeth Ardayfio-Sçhandorf (Ghana); Asmita Basu (India); Mary Ellsberg (United States of America); Sharmeen A. Farouk (Bangladesh); Dalia Farouki (Jordan); Dominique Fougeyrollas-Schwebel (France); Holly Johnson (Canada); Ivy Josiah (Malaysia); Sunita Kishor (India); Sami Nevala (Finland); Ruth Ojiambo Ochieng (Uganda); Ana Flávia d'Oliveira (Brazil); Patricia Tjaden (United States); Sylvia Walby (United Kingdom of Great Britain and Northern Ireland); and Jeanne Ward (Kenya/United States) (see http://www.un.org/womenwatch/daw/egm/vaw-stat-2005/index.html).

The second expert group meeting, on good practices, was organized in collaboration with the United Nations Office on Drugs and Crime (UNODC), with the participation of the following experts: Zarizana binti Abdul Aziz (Malaysia); Charlotte Bunch (United States); Ana Maria Carcedo Cabañas (Costa Rica); Sally Fay Goldfarb (United States); Claudia Hermannsdorfer Acosta (Honduras); Sheillah Kanyangarara (Zimbabwe); Elizabeth Kelly (United Kingdom); Fatma Aly Mostafa Khafagy (Egypt); Madhu Kishwar (India); Rosa Logar (Austria); Lori Michau (United States); Lepa Mladenovic (Serbia); Sapana Pradhan-Malla (Nepal); Leena Ruusuvuori (Finland);

and Lisa-Anne Vetten (South Africa) (see http://www.un.org/womenwatch/daw/egm/vaw-gp-2005/index.html). In both meetings, representatives of several entities of the United Nations system also participated.

Expert briefs were prepared by Alexis Aronowitz, Christine Chinkin, Katherine McKenna, Audra Bowlus and Tanis Day, Jørgen Lorentzen and Sylvia Walby.

Contributions to the study were provided by the International Center for Research on Women (Nata Duvvury and Caren Grown, with Subadra Panchanadeswaran and Katherine Weiland), Program for Appropriate Technology in Health (Mary Ellsberg), Elizabeth Schneider and Donna Sullivan (consultants) and staff of the Division for the Advancement of Women.

An advisory committee of 10 high-level, internationally recognized experts in the field of violence against women provided guidance and feedback on the approach, scope and content of the study, reviewed and commented on drafts and proposed a set of strategic recommendations. The members of the advisory committee were: Charlotte Bunch, Executive Director, Center for Women's Global Leadership (United States); Susana Chiarotti, former Regional Coordinator, Latin American and Caribbean Committee for the Defense of Women's Rights (Argentina); Dorcas Coker-Appiah, expert of the Committee on the Elimination of Discrimination against Women (Ghana); Radhika Coomaraswamy, former Special Rapporteur on violence against women, its causes and consequences and Special Representative of the Secretary-General on Children and Armed Conflict (Sri Lanka); Yakin Ertürk, Special Rapporteur on violence against women, its causes and consequences (Turkey); Alda Facio, former Director, Women, Gender and Justice Programme, United Nations Latin American Institute for the Prevention of Crime and the Treatment of Offenders (Costa Rica); Asma Khader, General Coordinator, Sisterhood Is Global Institute of Jordan and former counsel on violence against women to the Permanent Arab Court to Resist Violence Against Women (Jordan); Irene Khan, Secretary General, Amnesty International (Bangladesh), represented at meetings of the advisory committee by

Widney Brown; Angela Melo, Special Rapporteur on the Rights of Women in Africa, African Commission on Human and Peoples' Rights (Mozambique); and Heisoo Shin, expert of the Committee on the Elimination of Discrimination against Women (Republic of Korea).

A task force comprising entities of the United Nations system and non-governmental organizations (NGOs) provided inputs for the study and served as a channel for information exchange, consultations and awareness-raising. It included representatives of the following United Nations Secretariat bodies and United Nations funds, programmes and specialized agencies: Department of Peacekeeping Operations, Office for the Coordination of Humanitarian Affairs (OCHA), Office of the Special Adviser on Gender Issues and the Advancement of Women, United Nations Statistics Division, Office of the United Nations High Commissioner for Human Rights (OHCHR), UNODC, Economic Commission for Africa, Economic Commission for Europe, Economic Commission for Latin America and the Caribbean, Economic and Social Commission for Asia and the Pacific, Economic and Social Commission for Western Asia, United Nations Development Programme (UNDP), United Nations Development Fund for Women (UNIFEM), Office of the United Nations High Commissioner for Refugees (UNHCR), United Nations Human Settlements Programme (UN-Habitat), Joint United Nations Programme on HIV/AIDS (UNAIDS), United Nations Children's Fund (UNICEF), United Nations Population Fund (UNFPA), International Research and Training Institute for the Advancement of Women (INSTRAW), United Nations Interregional Crime and Justice Research Institute (UNICRI), International Labour Organization (ILO), United Nations Educational, Scientific and Cultural Organization (UNESCO), WHO and World Bank. The International Organization for Migration (IOM) was also part of the task force.

The task force also included the following non-governmental organizations: Amnesty International, Asia Pacific Forum on Women, Law and Development, Center for Reproductive Rights, Center for Women's Global Leadership, Latin American and Caribbean Committee for the Defense of Women's Rights (CLADEM), Equality Now, African Women's Development and Communication Network

(FEMNET), European Information Centre Against Violence (WAVE), Human Rights Watch (Women's Rights Division), International Gay and Lesbian Human Rights Commission, International Indigenous Women's Forum (MADRE), NGO Working Group on Women, Peace and Security, Open Society Institute (Network Women's Program), Women in Law and Development in Africa (WILDAF) and Women's Commission for Refugee Women and Children.

Ms. Edwina Sandys generously donated the use of her artwork "Oops," 1997, for the cover of this publication and other information materials related to the study.

Background material on the study is available at http://www.un.org/womenwatch/daw/vaw/index.htm.

CONTENTS

V. Collecting data on violence against women 65

Annex 1 171

■ Prevalence of physical assaults on women by a male partner

Annex 2 179

■ Costs of violence against women: selected studies generating a monetary estimate of costs

Violence against women persists in every country in the world as a pervasive violation of human rights and a major impediment to achieving gender equality. Such violence is unacceptable, whether perpetrated by the State and its agents or by family members or strangers, in the public or private sphere, in peacetime or in times of conflict. The Secretary-General has stated that as long as violence against women continues, we cannot claim to be making real progress towards equality, development and peace.

States have an obligation to protect women from violence, to hold perpetrators accountable and to provide justice and remedies to victims. Eliminating violence against women remains one of the most serious challenges of our time. The knowledge base and tools to prevent and eliminate violence against women developed over the past decade must be utilized more systematically and effectively to put a stop to all violence against women. This requires clear political will, outspoken, visible and unwavering commitment at the highest levels of leadership of the State and the resolve, advocacy and practical action of individuals and communities.

Significant work has been undertaken by States, entities of the United Nations system, NGOs, women's groups and networks and researchers to address male violence against women. The extensive work undertaken by different actors at different levels has led to a better understanding of the nature and scope of violence against women and an appreciation of its impact on women and on societies. International legal and policy frameworks for addressing such violence have been established, covering many different forms and types of violence in public as well as in private settings.

At the same time, much more remains to be done to create an environment where women can live free from gender-based violence.[1] Progress in the development of international legal norms, standards and policies has not been accompanied by comparable progress in their implementation at the national level, which remains insufficient and inconsistent in all parts of the world. Similarly, while data on the nature, prevalence and incidence of all forms of violence against women has increased significantly in recent years, information is not yet comprehensive. Lack of political will is reflected in inadequate resources devoted to tackling violence against women and a failure to create and maintain a political and social environment where violence against women is not tolerated. There is also a need to engage men more effectively in the work on preventing and eliminating such violence, and to tackle stereotypes and attitudes that perpetuate male violence against women.

The General Assembly has provided critical leadership in the global effort to combat violence against women. Its landmark Declaration on the Elimination of Violence against Women (resolution 48/104) provides the framework for analysis and action at the national and international levels. In recent years, the General Assembly has addressed violence against women in general, as well as specific forms and manifestations of such violence. These include violence against women migrant workers; trafficking in women and girls; traditional or customary practices affecting the health of women and girls; crimes against women committed in the name of "honour"; and domestic violence against women.

In December 2003, the General Assembly mandated—for the first time—the preparation of an in-depth study on all forms and manifestations of violence against women (resolution 58/185). This request is a clear signal of the importance that Member States—through the General Assembly—attach to addressing violence against women.

Specifically, the study aims to: highlight the persistence and unacceptability of all forms of violence against women in all parts of the world; strengthen the political commitment and joint efforts of all stakeholders to prevent and eliminate violence against women; and identify ways and means to ensure more sustained and effective implementation of State obligations to address all forms of violence against women, and to increase State accountability.

Scope of the study

Resolution 58/185 provides that the study should cover all forms and manifestations of violence against women, and include the following:

a. a statistical overview of all forms of violence against women, in order to better evaluate the scale of such violence while identifying gaps in data collection and formulating proposals for assessing the extent of the problem;

b. the causes of violence against women, including its root causes and other contributing factors;

c. the medium-term and long-term consequences of violence against women;

d. the health, social and economic costs of violence against women;

e. the identification of best practice examples in areas including legislation, policies, programmes and effective remedies and the efficiency of such mechanisms to the end of combating and eliminating violence against women.

It is not possible to discuss all forms and manifestations of violence against women comprehensively in one study. Rather, the present study endeavours to highlight and synthesize issues and concerns within the framework provided by resolution 58/185, with a view to supporting the work of the General Assembly. Some issues have recently been, or are being, addressed in other pertinent studies of the Secretary-General. The issue of violence against women in conflict and post-conflict situations was addressed in the study entitled "Women, peace and security" of 2002, prepared in response to Security Council resolution 1325 (2000). A study on violence against children is currently under preparation.

The present study sets out the broad context of violence against women and summarizes the knowledge base with regard to its extent and prevalence. It exposes the gaps and challenges in the availability of data, including methodologies for assessing the prevalence of such violence. It synthesizes causes and consequences, including costs. It discusses States' responsibility for preventing and addressing violence against women, and identifies promising practices and effective strategies for addressing it.

Section II of the present study gives a historical overview of the development of international awareness and action on male violence against women. It traces the processes and institutions that have been pivotal in categorizing such violence as a human rights concern. It summarizes the current framework for addressing violence against women contained in international and regional legal and policy instruments, including those agreed by global conferences of the United Nations. It gives attention to the role of the women's movement in raising awareness about such violence and the evolving challenges in addressing it.

Section III provides the historical and socio-cultural context within which violence against women occurs and persists. The section analyses the structural and systemic causes of male violence against women, in particular discrimination. It points to the role of patriarchy, denial of women's human rights, and male control over women's agency and sexuality. It highlights risk factors that increase women's vulnerability to violence, while also noting its universality and particularity, and factors that shape women's personal experience of such violence.

An overview of forms and manifestations of violence against women and its consequences is provided in section IV. It shows the continuum of violence against women throughout their lives and in a variety of settings. The section presents available evidence on the prevalence of different forms and manifestations of violence against women across countries. It assesses the consequences of such violence for the victim/survivor as well as for families, communities and nations, including the economic costs.

Section V outlines current progress and challenges in the collection of data and statistics on violence against women. It reviews available methodologies and their relevance for collection of particular types of data. It also notes the role of different actors in data collection. The section emphasizes the urgent need for enhanced data collection to strengthen the knowledge base on all forms of violence against women for informed policy and strategy development.

Section VI outlines the obligations of the State in preventing and eliminating all forms of violence against women, whether committed by State agents or non-State actors, protecting women from such violence and providing reparation to victims. It reviews applicable international norms and standards and the practice of judicial and other bodies in clarifying the content of States' responsibility to take action. It summarizes key actions to be taken towards meeting these obligations.

In section VII, promising practices in addressing violence against women are highlighted in three areas: the law, service provision and prevention. The section presents guiding principles that inform good or promising practice in these areas and gives illustrative examples. It also identifies a series of remaining challenges for implementing standards and norms on violence against women.

Section VIII draws conclusions and sets out recommendations for action, by different actors and at different levels, in seven key strategic areas.

Methodology

The study draws from existing research and knowledge at the national, regional and global levels. Among the many sources used are: contributions by Member States in response to a note verbale; responses of Member States to the questionnaire of the Secretariat for the 10-year review and appraisal of the implementation of the Beijing Declaration and Platform for Action, received in 2003 and 2004; reports of States parties under article 18 of the Convention on the Elimination of All Forms of Discrimination against Women; contributions by entities of the United Nations system, several human rights treaty bodies, and regional organizations; inputs by NGOs; and contributions made during an online discussion. Several consultations involving Member States and other stakeholders were held in 2005 and 2006, including in conjunction with the sixtieth session of the General Assembly and the fiftieth session of the Commission on the Status of Women, which also provided inputs. The study benefited from the comments and guidance of an advisory committee of 10 experts on violence against women from all regions. It also benefited from consultations with the independent expert for the Secretary-General's study on violence against children, Paulo Sérgio Pinheiro, and with the Special Rapporteur on violence against women, its causes and consequences.

The website of the Division for the Advancement of Women contains these and other resources, including a detailed bibliography and further information pertaining to legislation on different forms of violence against women (*see box 11*).

In this study, the term "violence against women" is understood to mean any act of gender-based violence that is directed against a woman because she is a woman or that affects women disproportionately (*see box 1 below*). It does not address gender-based violence suffered by men. The term "women" is used to cover females of all ages, including girls under the age of 18.

There is an ongoing debate over the use of the terms "victim" and "survivor", with some suggesting that the term "victim" should be avoided because it implies passivity, weakness and inherent vulnerability and fails to recognize the reality of women's resilience and agency. For others the term "survivor" is problematic because it denies the sense of victimization experienced by women who have been the target of violent crime. In this study, the term "victim" is generally used in the criminal justice context and the term "survivor" in the context of advocacy. At other points the term "victim/survivor" is used.■

II. OVERVIEW

Introduction

Violence against women has received growing attention at the United Nations as a form of discrimination and a violation of women's human rights. The international community has committed itself to protecting the rights and dignity of individual women and men through numerous treaties and declarations. Despite the increased attention to women's rights, there has been little progress in reducing violence against women. The present study concludes that violence against women has yet to receive the priority attention and resources needed at all levels to tackle it with the seriousness and visibility necessary. It seeks to provide evidence and recommendations that will assist Governments, intergovernmental institutions and civil society in addressing this question and in redressing this global injustice.

International attention: the women's movement and the United Nations

The issue of violence against women came to prominence because of the grass-roots work of women's organizations and movements around the world. As women sought to gain equality and recognition of their rights in many areas, they drew attention to the fact that violence against women was not the result of random, individual acts of misconduct, but was deeply rooted in structural relationships of inequality between women and men (*see sect. III*). In calling for action and redress for these violations nationally and internationally, women exposed the role of violence against women as a form of discrimination and a mechanism to perpetuate it. This process led to the identification of many different forms and manifestations of violence against women (*see sect. IV*), drawing them out of the private domain to public attention and the arena of State accountability.

At the international level, the issue of violence against women came onto the agenda in the context of women's rights activism at the United Nations. The interaction between women's advocacy around the world and United Nations initiatives over several decades has been a driving factor in achieving this attention. Some particular forms of violence against women, such as trafficking for forced prostitution, had been addressed before the founding of the United Nations.[2] However, wider attention to violence against women emerged primarily in the context of the United Nations Decade for Women (1976-1985), as more women's organizations became linked to the United Nations agenda through international and regional women's conferences and through women in development initiatives. Their efforts acted as a catalyst in expanding the understanding of violence against women. They supported the development of international norms and standards and the creation of monitoring and reporting mechanisms.[3]

Early initiatives to address violence against women at the international level focused primarily on the family. The World Plan of Action for Women,[4] adopted in 1975 at the World Conference of the International Women's Year in Mexico City, drew attention to the need for education programmes and ways to resolve family conflict that ensured dignity, equality and security to each family member, but did not explicitly refer to violence. However, the parallel NGO Tribunal held in Mexico City and the International Tribunal on Crimes against Women in Brussels in 1976 highlighted many more forms of violence against women.[5]

The 1980 Copenhagen mid-decade Second World Conference of the United Nations Decade for Women[6] adopted a resolution on violence in the family. It referred to violence in the home in its final report and, in the context of health care, called for the development of programmes to eliminate violence against women and children and to protect women from physical and mental abuse. Violence against women was also addressed in the parallel NGO forum and several Government delegations addressed this issue. This reflected its growing importance on the agendas of women's movements at the national level.[7]

Women's activism on violence against women increased in the early 1980s and the issue was more prominent at the Third World Conference on Women in Nairobi in 1985.[8] The Nairobi Forward-Looking Strategies for the Advancement of Women recognized the prevalence of violence against women in various forms in everyday life in all societies and identified diverse manifestations of violence by calling attention to abused women in the home, women victims of trafficking and involuntary prostitution, women in detention and women in armed conflict. The link between violence against women and other issues on the United Nations agenda began to be drawn as such violence was identified as a major obstacle to achieving the objectives of the Decade for Women: equality, development and peace. The Forward-Looking Strategies called for preventive policies, legal measures, national machinery and comprehensive assistance to women victims of violence. They also acknowledged the need for public awareness of violence against women as a societal problem.

Parallel to the work on violence against women in the framework of the Decade for Women, United Nations bodies dealing with crime prevention and criminal justice increasingly addressed violence against women, in particular domestic violence.[9] Work in this sector demonstrated that it was a significantly underreported global phenomenon that was committed in different contexts and highlighted the need for appropriate laws and access to justice for women victims, as well as effective implementation and enforcement of laws at the national level.[10]

During the early 1990s, efforts by the women's movement to gain recognition of violence against women as a human rights issue gained momentum. For the World Conference on Human Rights in Vienna in 1993, women caucused and lobbied globally and regionally to redefine the contours of human rights law to include the experiences of women. They presented conference delegates with almost half a million signatures from 128 countries demanding that such violence be recognized as a violation of women's human rights, and ran a global tribunal in which women's testimonies, including cases of violence from around the world, were presented in a human rights framework.[11]

Violence against women: a form of discrimination and human rights violation

Evidence gathered by researchers of the pervasive nature and multiple forms of violence against women, together with advocacy campaigns, led to the recognition that violence against women was global, systemic and rooted in power imbalances and structural inequality between men and women. The identification of the link between violence against women and discrimination was key.

The work of the Committee on the Elimination of Discrimination against Women, the treaty body established in 1982 to monitor implementation of the Convention on the Elimination of All Forms of Discrimination against Women,[12] contributed significantly to the recognition of violence against women as a human rights issue. The Convention does not explicitly refer to violence against women, but the Committee has made clear that all forms of violence against women fall within the definition of discrimination against women as set out in the Convention. The Committee regularly calls on States parties to adopt measures to address such violence. In its general recommendation No. 12 (1989),[13] the Committee noted States' obligation to protect women from violence under various articles of the Convention, and requested them to include information on the incidence of violence and the measures adopted to confront it in their periodic reports to the Committee. General recommendation No. 19 (1992)[14] decisively established the link: it asserted unequivocally that violence against women constitutes a form of gender-based discrimination and that discrimination is a major cause of such violence. This analysis brought the issue of violence against women within the terms of the Convention and the international legal norm of non-discrimination on the basis of sex and, thus, directly into the language, institutions and processes of human rights. The inquiry and individual complaints procedures under the Optional Protocol to the Convention, in force since 2000, allow the Committee to develop jurisprudence in this area (*see sect. VI*).

The World Conference on Human Rights in Vienna in 1993 saw a coordinated global mobilization to reaffirm women's rights as human rights. Women from all regions, from both Governments and NGOs, collaborated and organized to influence both regional and global preparatory processes for the Conference by campaigning to bring a gender perspective to the international human rights agenda and to increase the visibility of violations of women's human rights. The Vienna Declaration and Programme of Action included affirmation of the universality of women's rights as human rights and a call for elimination of gender-based violence. The Vienna Conference also added significant momentum to the adoption of the Declaration on the Elimination of Violence against Women[15] by the General Assembly later that year.

The Declaration on the Elimination of Violence against Women states that violence against women is "a manifestation of historically unequal power relations between men and women, which have led to domination over and discrimination against women by men and to the prevention of the full advancement of women".[16] It highlights the different sites of violence against women: violence in the family, violence in the community and violence perpetrated or condoned by the State. The Declaration is sensitive to the fact that particular groups of women are especially prone to be targeted for violence, including minority, indigenous and refugee women, destitute women, women in institutions or in detention, girls, women with disabilities, older women and women in situations of armed conflict. The Declaration sets out a series of measures to be taken by States to prevent and eliminate such violence. It requires States to condemn violence against women and not invoke custom, tradition or religion to avoid their obligations to eliminate such violence.

Box 1
Definitions of violence against women

General recommendation No. 19
Gender-based violence against women is "violence that is directed against a woman because she is a woman, or violence that affects women disproportionately. It includes acts that inflict physical, mental or sexual harm or suffering, threats of such acts, coercion and other deprivations of liberty."

"Gender-based violence, which impairs or nullifies the enjoyment by women of human rights and fundamental freedoms under general international law or under human rights conventions, is discrimination within the meaning of article 1 of the Convention." (Committee on the Elimination of Discrimination against Women general recommendation No. 19, para. 7)

Declaration on the Elimination of Violence against Women, article 1
Violence against women "means any act of gender-based violence that results in, or is likely to result in, physical, sexual or psychological harm or suffering to women, including threats of such acts, coercion or arbitrary deprivation of liberty, whether occurring in public or in private life." (General Assembly resolution 48/104)

General Assembly resolution on the Elimination of Domestic Violence against Women
Recognizes that "domestic violence can include economic deprivation and isolation and that such conduct may cause imminent harm to the safety, health or well-being of women." (General Assembly resolution 58/147)

A further outcome of the Vienna conference was the appointment by the Commission on Human Rights in 1994 of a Special Rapporteur on violence against women, its causes and consequences.[17] This mandate created an institutional mechanism for regular in-depth review and reporting on violence against women around the world.[18] The work is conducted within the framework of the international human rights regime and includes recommendations on how to eliminate violence against women and its causes and remedy its consequences. Through analysis, recommendations and country visits, the Special Rapporteur has raised awareness of the causes and consequences of different forms of violence against women and has further elaborated an understanding of international standards in this area.

The Beijing Declaration and Platform for Action, adopted by 189 countries at the Fourth World Conference on Women in Beijing in 1995, consolidated these gains by underlining that violence against women is both a violation of women's human rights and an impediment to the full enjoyment by women of all human rights. The focus shifted to demanding State accountability for action to prevent and eliminate violence against women. The Beijing Platform for Action identified 12 critical areas of concern that require urgent action to achieve the goals of equality, development and peace; one of these areas was on violence against women. Such violence is also addressed in several other critical areas of concern.[19]

At the five-year review of the Beijing Platform for Action in 2000, States specified that violence against women and girls, whether occurring in public or private life, is a human rights issue and highlighted State responsibility in addressing such violence.[20] Governments were asked to take all appropriate measures to eliminate discrimination and violence against women by any person, organization or enterprise and to treat all forms of violence against women and girls as criminal offences.

Security Council resolution 1325 (2000) on women and peace and security[21] was a milestone in addressing violence against women in situations of armed conflict. Recognizing the need to fully implement laws that protect the rights of women and girls during and after armed conflict, it calls for special measures to protect women and girls from gender-based violence in armed conflict. The resolution also emphasized the responsibility of all States to put an end to the impunity of perpetrators.

Consequences of addressing violence against women as a human rights concern

The first Special Rapporteur on violence against women described the violence against women movement as "perhaps the greatest success story of international mobilization around a specific human rights issue, leading to the articulation of international norms and standards and the formulation of international programmes and policies."[22]

There are important consequences that flow from categorizing violence against women as a matter of human rights. Recognizing violence against women as a violation of human rights clarifies the binding obligations on States to prevent, eradicate and punish such violence and their accountability if they fail to comply with these obligations. These obligations arise from the duty of States to take steps to respect, protect, promote and fulfil human rights. Claims on the State to take all appropriate measures to respond to violence against women thus move from the realm of discretion and become legal entitlements. The human rights framework provides access to a number of tools and mechanisms that have been developed to hold States accountable at the international and regional level. These include the human rights treaty bodies and international criminal tribunals, as well as the African, European and inter-American human rights systems (*see sect. VI*).

Human rights provide a unifying set of norms that can be used to hold States accountable for adhering to their obligations, to monitor progress and to promote coordination and consistency. Addressing violence against women as a human rights issue empowers women, positioning them not as passive recipients of discretionary benefits but as active rights-holders. It also enhances the participation of other human rights advocates, including men and boys, who become stake-holders in addressing violence against women as part of building respect for all human rights.

Recognizing violence against women as a human rights issue has also enabled human rights discourse and practice to become more inclusive by encompassing the experiences of women. When women's particular experiences remain invisible, they do not inform the under-standing of human rights violations and remedies for them.[23] Human rights norms therefore must take into account the particular circum-stances of women in order to be fully universal. An integrated and inclusive human rights regime should take into account not only gender perspectives but also the wide variety of factors that shape and reinforce women's, and men's, experiences of discrimination and violence, including race, ethnicity, class, age, sexual orientation, disability, nationality, religion and culture.

Understanding violence against women as a human rights con-cern does not preclude other approaches to preventing and eliminating violence, such as education, health, development and criminal justice efforts. Rather, addressing violence against women as a human rights issue encourages an indivisible, holistic and multisectoral response that adds a human rights dimension to work in all sectors. It calls for strengthening and accelerating initiatives in all areas to prevent and elim-inate violence against women, including in the criminal justice, health, development, humanitarian, peacebuilding and security sectors.

Integrating violence against women and expanding the scope of action

As the understanding of violence against women as a human rights issue evolved during the 1990s, so too did the implications of this violence for many different sectors. As a result, an increasing number of stakeholders now address the impact of violence against women in their goals and mandates. Similarly, the understanding of the scope and dimensions of violence against women continues to evolve through policy and practice, as reflected in the work of human rights treaty bodies and special procedures, international criminal tribunals, intergovernmental bodies and a range of United Nations entities and regional bodies.

Women-specific policies and programmes continue to drive the agenda on violence against women in the United Nations. At the same time, increased attention is being given to ensuring that women's right to be free from violence is protected in a comprehensive manner. Human rights treaty bodies increasingly integrate women's perspectives and experiences into the scope of their work and pay attention to violence against women within their mandates. The Human Rights Committee and the Committee on Economic, Social and Cultural Rights have, for example, adopted general comments on the equal right of men and women to the enjoyment of rights,[24] and the Committee on the Elimination of Racial Discrimination has adopted a general recommendation on the gender-related dimensions of racial discrimination.[25] These contain explicit references to the nature, scope and extent of violence against women and to States' responsibilities to prevent and eliminate it. Other treaty bodies also refer to the need to eliminate and prevent violence against women in their concluding observations on States parties' reports (*see sect. VI*).

In addition to the Special Rapporteur on violence against women, other thematic special rapporteurs of the Commission on Human Rights deal with violence-related issues. These include the Special Rapporteurs on sale of children, child prostitution and child pornography and on trafficking in persons, especially in women and children. Other special rapporteurs have also begun to address the impact of violence against women within their mandates, such as the Special Rapporteurs on torture and on the right to health, food, education, adequate housing, freedom of opinion and expression and freedom of religion or belief. The Special Rapporteur on extrajudicial, summary or arbitrary executions and the Special Rapporteur on the independence of judges and lawyers, have both focused on crimes against women committed in the name of "honour."

The General Assembly and the functional commissions of the Economic and Social Council have regularly addressed violence against women.[26] In particular, the Commission on the Status of Women, the Commission on Human Rights and its main subsidiary body, the Sub-Commission on the Promotion and Protection of Human Rights, and the Commission on Crime Prevention and Criminal Justice have adopted resolutions giving guidance on actions to be taken, at different levels and by different stakeholders, to prevent and eliminate specific forms of violence. Some resolutions have reinforced civil society initiatives, such as the General Assembly recognition in 1999 of 25 November as the International Day for the Elimination of Violence against Women.[27]

Intergovernmental conferences and summits have reaffirmed the commitment to eliminate violence against women. For example, the 1994 International Conference on Population and Development, held in Cairo, recognized that the elimination of violence against women is necessary for the empowerment of women.[28] At the Millennium Summit, held in 2000, Heads of State and Government resolved to combat all forms of violence against women.[29] The 2005 World Summit underlined the urgency of eliminating all forms of discrimination and violence against women and the girl child and linked this to the achievement of the Millennium Development Goals.[30]

The International Criminal Tribunals for the former Yugoslavia and for Rwanda, and the Special Court for Sierra Leone have enhanced the role of the international criminal justice system in providing accountability for violence against women in armed conflict. The Rome Statute of 1998 establishing the International Criminal Court includes several types of gender-based crimes (*see sect. VI*).

As a result of the directives to integrate a gender perspective into all areas of work in the United Nations, more policies and programmes seek to take into account the various impacts of their actions on women and men. The range of entities engaged in programmes to eliminate violence against women has grown.[31] These bodies contribute to research, normative and policy development, services and support to victims/survivors of violence, advocacy and awareness-raising activities and funding. While the number of United Nations bodies that now list violence against women as one of their concerns is impressive, the amount of resources and attention given to this issue is still small and the work lacks effective coordination.

Regional institutions have also addressed violence against women. Regional treaties include the Inter-American Convention on the Prevention, Punishment and Eradication of Violence against Women (Convention of Belém do Pará); the Protocol to the African Charter on Human and Peoples' Rights on the Rights of Women in Africa; and the South Asian Association for Regional Cooperation Convention on Preventing and Combating Trafficking in Women and Children for Prostitution (*see sect. VI*). Initiatives at the regional level in Africa include the special addendum on the eradication of all forms of violence against women and children (1998) to the 1997 Southern African Development Community's Declaration on Gender and Development and, at the European level, recommendation 2002 (5), issued by the Committee of Ministers of the Council of Europe to member States on the protection of women against violence.

These regional initiatives, which are informed by international standards on violence against women, establish regional mechanisms, including monitoring bodies, to prevent and eliminate such violence. Some regional initiatives expand on existing standards. For example, the Protocol to the African Charter on Human and Peoples' Rights on the Rights of Women in Africa expanded the definition in the Declaration on the Elimination of Violence against Women by including within its ambit economic violence or harm. The Convention of Belém do Pará asserts the right of women to be free from violence in both the public and private spheres and imposes a number of obligations on States in this regard. It also stresses the link between violence and women's enjoyment of all other rights.

Box 3
Preventing and responding to violence against women: the United Nations system

Within the United Nations system, a range of bodies, offices and agencies implement specific programmes on violence against women or include efforts to address such violence within their overall mandates and objectives. A survey of United Nations entities indicates that 32 of these undertake work on violence against women at the global, regional and national level. Such work covers many aspects of violence against women, from domestic and intimate partner violence to violence against women in conflict and post-conflict situations.

The work of United Nations entities also includes efforts to eliminate trafficking in women and to prevent sexual exploitation and abuse in each country where the United Nations has a presence, including by United Nations staff and other personnel. Increasing attention is being paid to the role of men and boys in preventing violence against women. The role of violence against women as an obstacle for development receives growing attention. Entities respond to the links between violence against women and other areas, such as HIV/AIDS, and contribute to data collection and the enhancement of the knowledge base on different forms and manifestations of violence against women.

Gaps and challenges persist, and efforts are needed to achieve a more comprehensive and well-coordinated system-wide response to violence against women, in particular with respect to:

- implementation of the legal and policy frameworks that guide United Nations system efforts to prevent and eliminate violence against women

- data collection and research

- awareness-raising, communication and dissemination of good practices

- coordinated response at the national level

- resource mobilization

- coordination mechanisms at the international level

A task force of the Inter-Agency Network on Women and Gender Equality of the United Nations system aims to enhance system-wide coordination and strengthen efforts to address violence against women. The Trust Fund in Support of Actions to Eliminate Violence against Women, managed by UNIFEM, supports innovative and catalytic projects around the world aimed at eliminating violence against women.

The Inter-Parliamentary Union has highlighted the role of parliaments in combating violence against women in all fields.[32] Many States have enacted legislation and developed policies and programmes to address violence against women.[33] Some States have adopted national action plans, which generally include support measures for victims/survivors; awareness-raising, education and sensitization; training and capacity-building; and the prosecution, punishment and rehabilitation of perpetrators. However, progress is uneven. Most countries still lack a coordinated multidisciplinary approach that includes the criminal justice system, health care and other services, the media and the education system.

The differing levels of activity to address violence against women in individual countries make it hard to assess the overall success of national efforts. Comparisons are made all the more difficult by the fact that the manifestations of violence against women vary according to the social, economic and historical context.[34] However, it is clear that violence against women remains a devastating reality in all parts of the world, and the implementation of international and regional standards to eradicate such violence is therefore an urgent priority. Strategies to stem this pandemic can draw on the variety of promising practices and strategies to address violence against women that have been implemented in countries around the world (*see sect. VII*).

Violence prevents women from contributing to, and benefiting from, development by restricting their choices and limiting their ability to act. The resulting consequences for economic growth and poverty reduction should be of central concern to Governments.[35] Violence against women also undermines and constrains the achievement of the Millennium Development Goals, including those set in the areas of poverty, education, child health, maternal mortality, HIV/AIDS and overall sustainable development.[36] Unless attention to preventing and redressing violence against women is incorporated in programmes to realize each of the Millennium Development Goals, the health, social and economic consequences of such violence can limit the potential benefits of these initiatives. Ultimately, the persistence of violence against women is inconsistent with all the Millennium Development Goals.[37]

Box 4
Guidelines on violence against women by the specialized agencies and other bodies of the United Nations

Inter-agency Standing Committee, *Guidelines for gender-based violence interventions in humanitarian settings: Focusing on prevention of and response to sexual violence in emergencies* (2006)
(http://www.humanitarianinfo.org/iasc/content/documents/subsidi/tf_gender/ IASC%20GBV%20Guidelines%20overview.PPT)

Secretary-General's *Bulletin on special measures for protection from sexual exploitation and sexual abuse* (2003) (ST/SGB/2003/13)

Office of the High Commissioner for Human Rights, Principles and Guidelines on Human Rights and Human Trafficking (2002)
(http://www.unhchr.ch/html/menu6/2/trafficking.doc)

UN-Habitat, *Safer Cities Programme, Guidelines for conducting safety audits* (Adapted for each city where audits are conducted. Information about the programme is available at: http://www.unhabitat.org/safercities)

United Nations High Commissioner for Refugees, *Guidelines for Prevention and Response: Sexual and gender-based violence against refugees, returnees and internally displaced persons* (2002)
(http://www.unhcr.org/cgi-bin/texis/vtx/protect/opendoc.pdf?tbl=PROTECTION&id=3f696bcc4)

United Nations High Commissioner for Refugees, *Guidelines on international protection, gender-related persecution within the context of Article 1 A (2) of the 1951 Convention and/or its 1967 Protocol relating to the status of refugees* (2002) (Available at:
http://www.unhcr.org/cgibin/texis/vtx/publ/opendoc.pdf?tbl=PUBL&id=3d58ddef4)

World Food Programme, *Executive Director's circulars on implementation of the Secretary-General's Bulletin on special measures for protection from sexual exploitation and sexual abuse*

World Health Organization, *Guidelines for medico-legal care for victims of sexual violence* (2003)
(http://www.who.int/violence_injury_prevention/publications/ violence/med_leg_guidelines/en/)

World Health Organization, *Ethical and safety guidelines for interviewing trafficked women* (2003)
(http://www.who.int/gender/documents/en/final%20recommenda-tions%2023%20oct.pdf)

World Health Organization, *Ethical and safety recommendations for domestic violence research* (1999)
(http://www.who.int/gender/violence/womenfirtseng.pdf)

Challenges and obstacles

Violence against women will not be eradicated without political will and commitment at the highest levels to make it a priority locally, nationally, regionally and internationally. Political will is expressed in a variety of ways, including legislation, national plans of action, adequate resource allocation, location of mechanisms to address violence against women at the highest levels, efforts to overcome impunity, visible condemnation of this violence, and sustained support by leaders and opinion makers of efforts to eradicate it. Creating an environment conducive to the effective functioning of NGOs working on this issue and collaboration with them are also indications of political will.

Promoting and protecting the human rights of women and strengthening efforts to achieve substantive equality between women and men are key to preventing violence against women. Structural imbalances of power and inequality between women and men are both the context and causes of violence against women (*see sect. III*). As the present study makes clear, the elimination of violence and discrimination against women in all spheres requires a comprehensive, coordinated and sustained effort. It requires action in different arenas, including legislation; the criminal justice sector; economic and social policies; services; awareness-raising and education.

A particularly problematic challenge is the elimination of discriminatory sociocultural attitudes and economic inequalities that reinforce women's subordinate place in society. Male violence against women is generated by sociocultural attitudes and cultures of violence in all parts of the world, and especially by norms about the control of female reproduction and sexuality (*see sect. III*). Furthermore, violence against women intersects with other factors, such as race and class, and with other forms of violence, including ethnic conflict.

The emergence in many places of a backlash against advances in the status of women has increased the difficulty of changing sociocultural attitudes that perpetuate impunity for violence against women. In come contexts, organized political forces, including different forms of cultural or religious "fundamentalisms", have put pressure on Governments to reverse advances in women's rights (*see sect. III*). Previous gains by women have been eroded or are under threat in some countries around the world.

Controversies over strategies and approaches have also emerged among those who seek to end violence against women. For example, there are disagreements over how best to counter trafficking in women, whether and when prostitution constitutes violence against women, and where to draw the line between a woman's freedom of choice and her victimization. Nevertheless, in spite of such controversies and complexities, the obligation of States to defend the human rights of women in all situations, including their right to freedom from violence against women, is clear (*see sect. VI*).

A serious obstacle to progress is the inadequate and uneven data on various forms of violence against women and on how they affect different groups of women. The lack of data to evaluate the measures taken impedes informed analysis and policymaking, which are critical to developing the most effective responses (*see sect. IV*).

Overcoming these challenges requires dedicated and sustained resources. Although many of the required actions are not resource-intensive—for example, adopting the necessary legislation—even these actions are often not carried out (*see sects. IV and VII and box 11*). The question remains why even those steps are not taken and why so few resources are committed to an issue that harms so many. For example, 10 years after its creation, the United Nations Trust Fund to End Violence against Women only receives less than $2 million a year. Funding measures to end violence against women should be a higher priority for both Governments and donors.

Eliminating societal attitudes and structures that support and perpetuate systemic discrimination and violence against women requires coordinated and multifaceted efforts by Governments, NGOs and other actors. The challenge is to create an integrated and coordinated strategy that combines targeted initiatives for the promotion of gender equality, including the elimination of violence against women, with systematic use of the gender mainstreaming strategy in all sectors. Such efforts need to be supported by strong women-specific mechanisms that enhance coordination and function as a catalyst for action.

Women's movements and human rights organizations have a crucial role to play in initiatives to address violence against women, in particular to translate international standards into reality at the local level. At the national level, women's rights activists and NGOs continue to use international standards and norms on the elimination of violence against women as lobbying tools and benchmarks for assessing government efforts to prevent, eliminate and redress such violence.

Despite the complexities and challenges, progress towards ending violence against women has begun, and there are many initiatives and recommendations pointing the way forward. Bold leadership on the elimination of violence against women at every level of society, together with increased political will and the allocation of significant resources, can lead to a dramatic reduction of such violence.

Box 5
Selected instruments of law, policy and practice on violence against women

International treaties

Convention on the Elimination of All Forms of Discrimination against Women

Optional Protocol to the Convention on the Elimination of All Forms of Discrimination against Women

International Covenant on Civil and Political Rights and Optional Protocol

International Covenant on Economic, Social and Cultural Rights

International Convention on the Elimination of All Forms of Racial Discrimination

Convention against Torture and Other Cruel, Inhuman or Degrading Treatment or Punishment

Convention on the Rights of the Child and Optional Protocols

International Convention on the Protection of the Rights of All Migrant Workers and Members of Their Families

Protocol to Prevent, Suppress and Punish Trafficking in Persons, Especially Women and Children, supplementing the United Nations Convention against Transnational Organized Crime

Rome Statute of the International Criminal Court

Geneva Convention relative to the Protection of Civilian Persons in Times of War (Fourth Geneva Convention)

Box 5 (*cont'd*)

Regional treaties

Inter-American Convention on the Prevention, Punishment and Eradication of Violence against Women (Convention of Belém do Pará)

Protocol to the African Charter on Human and Peoples' Rights on the Rights of Women in Africa

South Asian Association for Regional Cooperation Convention on Preventing and Combating Trafficking in Women and Children for Prostitution

International policy instruments

Vienna Declaration and Programme of Action, adopted at the World Conference on Human Rights

Programme of Action of the International Conference on Population and Development

Beijing Declaration and Platform for Action, adopted at the Fourth World Conference on Women

Outcome document of the twenty-third special session of the General Assembly entitled: "Women 2000: Gender equality, development and peace for the twenty-first century" (General Assembly resolution S-23/3)

Selected recent General Assembly resolutions

Declaration on the Elimination of Violence against Women, resolution 48/104

Crime prevention and criminal justice measures to eliminate violence against women, resolution 52/86

United Nations Millennium Declaration, resolution 55/2, particularly para. 25.

Traditional or customary practices affecting the health of women and girls, resolution 56/128

Elimination of domestic violence against women, resolution 58/147

Working towards the elimination of crimes against women and girls committed in the name of honour, resolution 59/165

Trafficking in women and girls, resolution 59/166

Violence against women migrant workers, resolution 60/139

2005 World Summit Outcome, resolution 60/1, particularly para. 58 (f).

Security Council resolution

Resolution 1325 (2000) on women and peace and security

Commission on Human Rights resolution (most recent)[a]

Elimination of violence against women, resolution 2005/41

United Nations treaty bodies

Committee on the Elimination of Discrimination against Women: general recommendation No. 12, violence against women

Committee on the Elimination of Discrimination against Women: general recommendation No. 14, female circumcision

Committee on the Elimination of Discrimination against Women: general recommendation No. 19, violence against women

Committee on the Elimination of Racial Discrimination: general recommendation No. 25, gender related dimensions of racial discrimination

Human Rights Committee: general comment No. 28, equality of rights between men and women (article 3)

Committee on Economic, Social and Cultural Rights: general comment No. 14, the right to the highest attainable standard of health

Committee on Economic, Social and Cultural Rights: general comment No. 16, the equal right of men and women to the enjoyment of all economic, social and cultural rights (article 3)

Inter-Parliamentary Union

How Parliaments can and must promote effective ways of combating violence against women in all fields, resolution of 12 May 2006

---

[a] General Assembly resolution 60/251 established the Human Rights Council. It also transferred to the Council all existing mandates, mechanisms, functions and responsibilities of the Commission on Human Rights. The resolution also extended these mandates by one year within which the Council is to complete a review.

III. THE CONTEXT AND CAUSES OF VIOLENCE AGAINST WOMEN

Introduction

The recognition of violence against women as a form of discrimination and, thus, a human rights violation, provides an entry point for understanding the broad context from which such violence emerges and related risk factors. The central premise of the analysis of violence against women within the human rights framework is that the specific causes of such violence and the factors that increase the risk of its occurrence are grounded in the broader context of systemic gender-based discrimination against women and other forms of subordination. Such violence is a manifestation of the historically unequal power relations between women and men reflected in both public and private life.[38] The human rights-based approach reveals the scope of women's inequality and points to the linkages between violations of a range of women's human rights, including violence against women. It highlights the link between the realization of women's rights and the elimination of power disparities. Vulnerability to violence is understood as a condition created by the absence or denial of rights.

Violence against women is not confined to a specific culture, region or country, or to particular groups of women within a society. The different manifestations of such violence and women's personal experience of it are, however, shaped by many factors, including economic status, race, ethnicity, class, age, sexual orientation, disability, nationality, religion and culture. In order to prevent violence against women, the underlying root causes of such violence and the effects of the intersection of the subordination of women and other forms of social, cultural, economic and political subordination, need to be identified and addressed.

The causes of violence against women have been investigated from diverse perspectives, including feminism, criminology, development, human rights, public health and sociology. Various explanations have emerged from these empirical and theoretical inquiries. While they differ in the emphasis given to individual and societal factors in explaining violence against women, all have concluded that no single cause adequately accounts for violence against women.[39] Such violence arises from the convergence of specific factors within the broad context of power inequalities at the individual, group, national and global levels.

The human rights-based approach encourages a holistic and multisectoral response to violence against women. It permits an understanding of the interrelationships between women's human rights and how denial of these rights creates the conditions for violence against them. Human rights establish the State's obligations to address the causes of violence against women, and to prevent and respond to all violence against women, including that committed by non-State actors, and hold States accountable for the fulfilment of these obligations.[40] Human rights also encourage communities to examine practices and values that promote violence against women and offer guidance for sustainable change.[41]

The broad context and structural causes of violence against women

Patriarchy and other relations of dominance and subordination

Violence against women is both universal and particular. It is universal in that there is no region of the world, no country and no culture in which women's freedom from violence has been secured. The pervasiveness of violence against women across the boundaries of nation, culture, race, class and religion points to its roots in patriarchy - the systemic domination of women by men. The many forms and manifestations of violence and women's differing experiences of violence point to the intersection between gender-based subordination and other forms of subordination experienced by women in specific contexts.

Historically, gender roles—the socially constructed roles of women and men—have been ordered hierarchically, with men exercising power and control over women. Male dominance and female subordination have both ideological and material bases. Patriarchy has been entrenched in social and cultural norms, institutionalized in the law and political structures and embedded in local and global economies. It has also been ingrained in formal ideologies and in public discourse. Patriarchy restricts women's choices but does not render women powerless, as evidenced by the existence of women's movements and successful claims by women for their rights.

Patriarchy has had different historical manifestations and it functions differently in specific cultural, geographic and political settings. It is intertwined with other systems of subordination and exclusion. It is shaped by the interaction of a wide range of factors, including histories of colonialism and post-colonial domination, nation-building initiatives, armed conflict, displacement and migration. Its expressions are also influenced by economic status, race, ethnicity, class, age, sexual orientation, disability, nationality, religion and culture. Analysis of the gender-based inequalities that give rise to violence must therefore take into account the specific factors that disempower women in a particular setting.[42] Such contextualized analyses of women's experiences of violence reveal that women exercise agency and varying degrees of control over their lives even within the constraints of multiple forms of subordination.[43]

A number of key means through which male dominance and women's subordination are maintained are common to many settings. These include: exploitation of women's productive and reproductive work; control over women's sexuality and reproductive capacity; cultural norms and practices that entrench women's unequal status; State structures and processes that legitimize and institutionalize gender inequalities; and violence against women. Violence against women is both a means by which women's subordination is perpetuated and a consequence of their subordination.

Violence against women serves as a mechanism for maintaining male authority. When a woman is subjected to violence for transgressing social norms governing female sexuality and family roles, for example, the violence is not only individual but, through its punitive and controlling functions, also reinforces prevailing gender norms. Acts of violence against women cannot be attributed solely to individual psychological factors or socio-economic conditions such as unemployment. Explanations for violence that focus primarily on individual behaviours and personal histories, such as alcohol abuse or a history of exposure to violence, overlook the broader impact of systemic gender inequality and women's subordination. Efforts to uncover the factors that are associated with violence against women should therefore be situated within this larger social context of power relations.

People's perceptions of the causes of violence may or may not encompass these structural factors. In a 2005 study on intimate partner violence in Malawi, for example, researchers found that while most women identified social and cultural norms as major causal factors for the violence, including the practices of polygamy, wife inheritance and bride price, most men attributed violence largely to individual inter-personal dynamics.[44]

Violence against women also operates as a mechanism for maintaining the boundaries of both male and female gender roles. The norms governing these roles may be expressed in moral codes or in widely held social expectations. According to a WHO assessment on intimate partner violence and HIV/AIDS, "men use violence against women as a way of disciplining women for transgressions of traditional female roles or when they perceive challenges to their masculinity."[45] Intimate partner violence is significantly correlated with rigid gender roles that associate masculinity with dominance, toughness, male authority in the home and threats to male authority.[46]

Impunity for violence against women compounds the effects of such violence as a mechanism of control. When the State fails to hold the perpetrators accountable, impunity not only intensifies the subordination and powerlessness of the targets of violence, but also sends a message to society that male violence against women is both acceptable and inevitable. As a result, patterns of violent behaviour are normalized.

The relationship between violence against women and patriarchy was highlighted in a landmark decision by the Constitutional Court of South Africa in 1999. The Court found that the South African Constitution imposed a direct obligation on the State to provide protection from domestic violence. The Court linked this right to protection to the right to equality and non-discrimination.[47] Judge Albie Sachs explained that "to the extent that it is systemic, pervasive and overwhelmingly gender-specific, domestic violence *both reflects and reinforces patriarchal domination*, and does so in a particularly brutal form".[48]

Culture and violence against women

While some cultural norms and practices empower women and promote women's human rights, customs, traditions and religious values are also often used to justify violence against women. Certain cultural norms have long been cited as causal factors for violence against women, including the beliefs associated with "harmful traditional practices" (such as female genital mutilation/cutting, child marriage and son preference), crimes committed in the name of "honour", discriminatory criminal punishments imposed under religiously based laws, and restrictions on women's rights in marriage.[49] However, the cultural bases of other forms of violence against women have not been adequately examined, at least in part because of narrow conceptions of what constitutes "culture."

Culture is formed by the values, practices and power relations that are interwoven into the daily lives of individuals and their communities.[50] Social behaviour is mediated by culture in all societies and culture affects most manifestations of violence everywhere. But the particular relationship between culture and violence against women can only be clarified in specific historical and geographic contexts. Since culture is constantly being shaped and reshaped by processes of material and ideological change at the local and global levels, the capacity to change is essential to the continuation of cultural identities and ideologies.[51] Culture cannot be reduced to a static, closed set of beliefs and practices.

Culture is not homogenous. It incorporates competing and contradictory values. Particular values and norms acquire authority when political, economic and social developments bring their proponents to power or positions of influence. Determinations of what needs to be preserved change over time, as, for example, when male leaders willingly accept technology that massively affects culture, but resist changes in women's status, reflecting a tendency to treat women as the repositories of cultural identity.[52] Women are also actors in constituting culture: they "influence and build the cultures around them, changing them as they resist, and reinforcing and recreating them as they conform".[53] Key aspects of women's individual identities are interwoven with their cultural communities and their participation in cultural customs and practices. Women not only suffer from negative aspects of the cultures in which they live, they also benefit from and are supported by positive cultural values and practices within their communities.

Cultural justifications for restricting women's human rights have been asserted by some States and by social groups within many countries claiming to defend cultural tradition. These defences are generally voiced by political leaders or traditional authorities, not by those whose rights are actually affected.[54] Cultural relativist arguments have been advanced in national contexts and in international debates when laws and practices that curtail women's human rights have been challenged.[55] The politicization of culture in the form of religious "fundamentalisms" in diverse geographic and religious contexts has become a serious challenge to efforts to secure women's human rights.[56]

Tension between cultural relativism and the recognition of women's human rights, including the right to be free from violence, has been intensified as a result of the current heightened attention to State security issues. The resort to cultural relativism has been "made worse by the policies adopted since 11 September 2001 by many groups and societies that feel threatened and under siege".[57] This tension poses a notable challenge in ensuring that violence against women is kept firmly on the international and national agendas with the priority it requires.

The ways in which culture shapes violence against women are as varied as culture itself. For example, the phenomena of "date rape" and eating disorders are tied to cultural norms but are not often labelled as cultural phenomena. In the United States of America, researchers report high rates of violence against women in casual and longer-term romantic dating relationships, which are a culturally specific form of social relations between women and men, with culturally constructed expectations. According to one agency "40 per cent of teenage girls ages 14 to 17 say they know someone their age who has been hit or beaten by a boyfriend [and] one of five college females will experience some form of dating violence".[58] Eating disorders, including starvation dieting (anorexia) and bulimia (binge eating), are similarly tied to cultural values: "studies show expectation of body weight and appearance, particularly oriented towards girls, come from parents, peers, the dieting industry and images in the media".[59]

Various manifestations of femicide, the murder of women because they are women, illustrate the interrelationship between cultural norms and the use of violence in the subordination of women. Femicide takes place in many contexts: intimate partner violence, armed conflict, workplace harassment, dowry disputes and the protection of family "honour". For example, crimes committed in the name of "honour", usually by a brother, father, husband or other male family member, are a means of controlling women's choices, not only in the area of sexuality but also in other aspects of behaviour, such as freedom of movement. Such crimes frequently have a collective dimension, with the family as a whole believing itself to be injured by a woman's actual or perceived behaviour.[60] They are often public in character, which is integral to their social functions, which include influencing the conduct of other women. In other cultural contexts, preoccupation with women's sexuality is manifested not only in practices for enforcing chastity but also in the way female sexuality is turned into a commodity in the media and advertising.

The role of culture as a causal factor for violence against women must therefore be investigated within diverse cultural settings, taking into account the many ways in which the concept of culture is used. Culture can be most usefully viewed as a shifting set of discourses, power relations and social, economic and political processes, rather than as a fixed set of beliefs and practices. Given the fluidity of culture, women's agency in challenging oppressive cultural norms and articulating cultural values that respect their human rights is of central importance.[61] Efforts to address the impact of culture on violence should therefore take direction from the women who are seeking to ensure their rights within the cultural communities concerned.

Economic inequalities and violence against women

Economic inequalities can be a causal factor for violence against women both at the level of individual acts of violence and at the level of broad-based economic trends that create or exacerbate the enabling conditions for such violence.[62] These economic inequalities can be found at the local, national and global level. Women's economic inequalities and discrimination against women in areas such as employment, income, access to other economic resources and lack of economic independence reduce women's capacity to act and take decisions, and increase their vulnerability to violence.

Despite overall advances in women's economic status in many countries, many women continue to face discrimination in formal and informal sectors of the economy, as well as economic exploitation within the family. Women's lack of economic empowerment, also reflected in lack of access to and control over economic resources in the form of land, personal property, wages and credit, can place them at increased risk of violence. In addition, restrictions on women's control over economic resources, such as household income, can constitute a form of violence against women in the family. While economic independence does not shield women from violence, access to economic resources can enhance women's capacity to make meaningful choices, including escaping violent situations and accessing mechanisms for protection and redress.

Policies such as structural adjustment, deregulation of economies and privatization of the public sector have tended to reinforce women's economic and social inequality, especially within marginalized communities. Economic restructuring has reduced the capacity of many national Governments to promote and ensure women's rights through public sector programmes and social spending.[63]

WHO has noted the disruptive effects of globalization on social structures and consequent increases in overall levels of violence in society: "societies with already high levels of inequality, which experience a further widening of the gap between rich and poor as a result of globalization, are likely to witness an increase in interpersonal violence. Rapid social change in a country in response to strong global pressures—as occurred, for instance, in some of the states of the former Soviet Union—can overwhelm existing social controls over behaviour and create conditions for a high level of violence."[64] Since many existing social controls already rationalize or endorse various forms of violence against women, the social changes triggered by globalization in many contexts have tended to produce new forms or worsened existing forms of violence against women, including trafficking on a global scale.[65]

The large-scale inequities and upheavals associated with globalization exacerbate the conditions that generate violence against women by amplifying disparities of wealth and social privilege and impoverishing rural economies. They can also expose women to violence in the form of exploitative working conditions in inadequately regulated industries. At the same time, industrialization and economic migration offer women waged work outside the traditional boundaries of gender roles within their communities. The destabilization of traditional gender roles coexists with new permutations of gender subordination, however, and women are employed primarily in sex-segregated and low-wage industries.[66]

The current Special Rapporteur on violence against women has noted that while women's migration as workers or as "members of transnational households has the potential to empower women and give them direct access to international human rights law, opposing trends have also been observed. Some local and 'traditional' forms of violence against women have become globalized and others such as trafficking have become increasingly prevalent".[67] In many countries, women migrants also face discrimination based on race, ethnicity or national origin, little or no access to social services and increased domestic violence. Women who are undocumented or who do not have legal migration status are at even greater risk of violence and have even less access to protection or redress.[68]

Causal and risk factors for violence against women

Within the broad context of women's subordination, a number of specific causal factors for violence can be identified. These include structural causal factors such as the use of violence in conflict resolution, doctrines of privacy and State inaction, discussed below.[69] They also include individual or family behaviour patterns that create a higher risk of violence, also discussed below.

Use of violence in conflict resolution

A correlation between broad-based social and political acceptance of violence as a means of conflict resolution and violence against women can be traced at the individual, community and national levels. At the individual level, approaches to conflict resolution between couples and within families and interpersonal relationship skills are factors in determining whether conflict escalates into violence. At the community level, social norms governing how conflicts within the family or in the community should be handled create an environment that either condones or discourages violence.

At the national and international levels, the use of force to resolve political and economic disputes generates violence against women in armed conflict. The use of rape as a tool of war and atrocities targeting women are the most systematic expressions of violence against women in armed conflict. Control of women's sexuality and reproduction through systematic attacks against women has become a means of ethnic cleansing. For example, the use of rape and other forms of sexual violence in Kosovo (former Serbia and Montenegro) in 1999 as weapons of warfare and methods of ethnic cleansing had been preceded by official state propaganda and media accounts that stereotyped Kosovar Albanian women as sexually promiscuous and exploited Serbian fears of Albanian population growth.[70] The relationship between broad-based social and political acceptance of violence as a means of conflict resolution and violence against women is a critical area for further research.

Doctrines of privacy

Legal doctrines protecting the privacy of the home and family have been widely used to justify the failure of the State and society to intervene when violence is committed against women in the family and to take remedial action.[71] Deference to the privacy of the home, in both law and practice, contributes not only to impunity for violence against women at the hands of family members, but also to impunity for violence against domestic workers. The development of international law in the last 15 years has extended the State's human rights obligations in the family arena and States have adopted laws and policies in line with these obligations (*see sect. VI*). However, enforcement remains a pervasive challenge, as social norms and legal culture often protect privacy and male dominance within the family at the expense of the safety of women and girls.

State inaction

The State plays a key part in the construction and maintenance of gender roles and power relations. State inaction leaves in place discriminatory laws and policies that undermine women's human rights and disempowers women. It shifts responsibility for preventive and remedial measures to NGOs and other groups in civil society. It also functions as approval of the subordination of women that sustains violence and acquiescence in the violence itself. State inaction with regard to the proper functioning of the criminal justice system has particularly corrosive effects as impunity for acts of violence against women encourages further violence and reinforces women's subordination. Such inaction by the State to address the causes of violence against women constitutes lack of compliance with human rights obligations (*see sect. VI*).

Risk factors for violence

Major systemic causes often converge with other factors that may increase the risk of violence against women. Public health researchers have identified a number of factors that are correlated with, or are considered risk factors for, certain forms of violence. These include social and economic status, individual histories of exposure to violence, and individual types of behaviour. Studies conducted mostly in developed countries have focused primarily on intimate partner violence, childhood sexual abuse and sexual assault and rape by strangers. The data collected from these studies points to a recurring set of factors correlated statistically with violence against women, but these have not been established as direct causal factors.

A range of studies[72] identify risk factors at the levels of the individual, family, community, society and State. These have been summarized in one public health model and include:

a. At the level of the individual: youth; a history of abuse as a child; witnessing marital violence in the home; the frequent use of alcohol and drugs; low educational or economic status; and membership in marginalized and excluded communities. These factors are associated with both the perpetrators and victims/survivors of violence.

b. At the level of the couple and family: male control of wealth and decision-making authority within the family; a history of marital conflict; and significant interpersonal disparities in economic, educational or employment status.

c. At the level of the community: women's isolation and lack of social support; community attitudes that tolerate and legitimize male violence; and high levels of social and economic disempowerment, including poverty.

d.   At the level of society: gender roles that entrench male dominance and female subordination; and tolerance of violence as a means of conflict resolution.

e.   At the level of the State: inadequate laws and policies for the prevention and punishment of violence; and limited awareness and sensitivity on the part of law enforcement officials, courts and social service providers.

These analyses point to power disparities based on discrimination and inequalities as the underlying determinants of violence against women. As a leading researcher on domestic violence noted, although such violence "is greatest in relationships and communities where the use of violence in many situations is normative, notably when witnessed in childhood, *it is substantially a product of gender inequality and the lesser status of women compared with men in society.*"[73] A number of the risk factors cited above are tied to human rights violations. For example, girls and young women face violations of a range of rights guaranteed by the Convention on the Rights of the Child. Some of these violations constitute forms of violence and others increase the risk of violence.

Researchers have consistently found that poor women are at increased risk of intimate partner violence and sexual violence, including rape. However, when identifying poverty as a correlate or risk factor for violence against women, focus needs to be placed on the human rights dimensions of poverty. The correlation between poverty and violence against women points to the need for changes in policies and practices in order to respect, protect and fulfil women's economic and social rights. Emphasis thus moves beyond interventions at the individual level to address the structural factors that contribute to violence against women, including gender-based discrimination in access to resources and services and the denial of women's economic and social rights.

Implications for State and intergovernmental action

The centrality of discrimination against women and women's subordination as a cause of violence against women has clear implications for action by States and intergovernmental organizations. To meet their human rights obligations, States must take up the challenge of transforming the social and cultural norms regulating the relations of power between men and women and other linked systems of subordination. States have a responsibility to act as a catalyst for social change and cannot defer this responsibility to civil society groups. Historically, States have shaped cultural and social norms through laws and policies that incorporated existing gender relations of power or modified them to respond to State-centred goals, such as expanding the participation of women in the labour force. The question, therefore, is not whether States can and should play a role in transforming discriminatory social and cultural norms, but how they can do so most effectively. As a former Special Rapporteur on freedom of religion or belief emphasized: "[i]t is not the role of the State simply to keep abreast of society or stand for the social status quo. The State is also responsible for prompting and guiding change. The law does not need to be restricted to articulating the current situation. It can also be looked upon as an important vehicle for change, one whose power can be mobilized to wear down resistance and encourage the emergence of new mindsets, attitudes and ways of behaving."[74]

All efforts—State, intergovernmental and non-governmental—to address systemic gender-based discrimination against women must engage women in the communities concerned to provide leadership and develop strategies.[75] In this regard, State and intergovernmental organizations can draw on innovative approaches developed by civil society groups in community dialogue, awareness-raising and mobilization initiatives. Open and transparent collaboration between Government and those in civil society who oppose violence against women enhance such efforts (*see sect. VII*).[76]

The growing powers of transnational actors, including multinational corporations, political groups and criminal networks, have significant effects on women's economic and social rights.[77] These effects are not always adequately addressed in national law, resulting in gaps in accountability for violence against women and its causes. States and intergovernmental organizations should examine the role of these actors in generating violence against women, in order to devise appropriate responses. ■

IV. FORMS, CONSEQUENCES AND COSTS OF VIOLENCE AGAINST WOMEN

Introduction

Violence against women takes many different forms, manifested in a continuum of multiple, interrelated and sometimes recurring forms.[78] It can include physical, sexual and psychological/emotional violence and economic abuse and exploitation, experienced in a range of settings, from private to public, and in today's globalized world, transcending national boundaries. Naming forms and manifestations of violence against women is an important step towards recognizing and addressing them.

Forms and manifestations of violence against women vary depending on the specific social, economic, cultural and political context. Some forms of violence may grow in importance while others diminish as societies undergo demographic changes, economic restructuring and social and cultural shifts. For example, new technologies may generate new forms of violence, such as Internet or mobile telephone stalking. Consequently, no list of forms of violence against women can be exhaustive. States must acknowledge the evolving nature of violence against women and respond to new forms as they are recognized.

Violence against women has far-reaching consequences for women, their children and community and society as a whole. Women who experience violence suffer a range of health problems and their ability to earn a living and to participate in public life is diminished. Their children are significantly more at risk for health problems, poor school performance and behavioural disturbances.

The costs of violence against women, apart from the human costs, go beyond lowered economic production and reduced human capital formation but also include the costs associated with political and social instability through intergenerational transmission of violence, as well as the funds required for programmes for victims/survivors of violence.

Although most cases of violence against women involve a female victim/survivor and a male perpetrator, women also commit acts of violence. While women commit a small proportion of intimate partner violence, they are involved to a greater degree in the perpetration of harmful traditional practices and in trafficking. They have also engaged in acts of violence against women and children in the context of armed conflicts.

Forms and manifestations of violence against women in various settings

Ten years after the Beijing Platform for Action called for improved research and data collection on different forms of violence against women, the available evidence remains uneven and at times non-existent, although there has been notable progress, especially in regard to intimate partner violence (*see sect. V*). While rigorously evaluated data on the prevalence of violence against women may be limited for some forms of violence and lacking for others, the occurrence of acts of violence against women is well documented. In addition to surveys, information sources include States through reports to United Nations treaty bodies and other mechanisms, researchers, the media and NGOs.

The Declaration on the Elimination of Violence against Women and the Beijing Platform for Action address violence against women according to the site, or setting, where it occurs: in the family; within the general community; and perpetrated or condoned by the State. Many forms of violence against women occur in more than one setting: for example, harmful traditional practices that involve both the family and the community and are condoned by the State. Trafficking is a form of violence against women that involves family, community and State and crosses international boundaries. Violence against women in situations of armed conflict also extends into different settings. Different forms of violence against women may be linked, or reinforce one another. A range of factors also influence what forms of violence women suffer and how they experience it.

Violence against women within the family

The forms of violence a woman may experience within the family across her life cycle extend from violence before birth to violence against older women. Commonly identified forms of violence against women in the family include: battering and other forms of intimate partner violence including marital rape; sexual violence; dowry-related violence; female infanticide; sexual abuse of female children in the household; female genital mutilation/cutting and other traditional practices harmful to women; early marriage; forced marriage; non-spousal violence; violence perpetrated against domestic workers; and other forms of exploitation. There is more research and data available on intimate partner violence and on some forms of harmful practices than on many other forms and manifestations of violence against women.

Intimate partner violence

The most common form of violence experienced by women globally is intimate partner violence. The pervasiveness of different forms of violence against women within intimate relationships, commonly referred to as domestic violence or spousal abuse, is now well established. There is a growing body of research on intimate partner violence, which has expanded to capture the experience of women in intimate relationships beyond formal marriage.

Intimate partner violence includes a range of sexually, psychologically and physically coercive acts used against adult and adolescent women by a current or former intimate partner, without her consent.[79] Physical violence involves intentionally using physical force, strength or a weapon to harm or injure the woman. Sexual violence includes abusive sexual contact, making a woman engage in a sexual act without her consent, and attempted or completed sex acts with a woman who is ill, disabled, under pressure or under the influence of alcohol or other drugs. Psychological violence includes controlling or isolating the woman, and humiliating or embarrassing her. Economic violence includes denying a woman access to and control over basic resources.[80]

Population-based studies to document the scope and prevalence of intimate partner violence have been conducted in 71 countries around the world (*see annex 1*). In the WHO multi-country study on domestic violence,[81] implemented in Bangladesh, Brazil, Ethiopia, Japan, Namibia, Peru, Samoa, the former Serbia and Montenegro, Thailand and the United Republic of Tanzania, the lifetime prevalence of physical violence by an intimate partner ranged between 13 per cent and 61 per cent. In most of the sites surveyed, the range was between 23 and 49 per cent. The lifetime prevalence of sexual violence by an intimate partner was between 6 per cent and 59 per cent.[82] A previous review of 50 population-based studies in 36 countries showed that the lifetime prevalence of physical violence by intimate partners ranged between 10 per cent and over 50 per cent.[83] Most recently, a study in the Syrian Arab Republic revealed that 21.8 per cent of women had experienced some form of violence in the family and, of these, 48 per cent had been beaten (*see box 7*).[84]

At its most severe, intimate partner violence leads to death. Studies of femicide from Australia, Canada, Israel, South Africa and the United States of America show that 40 to 70 per cent of female murder victims were killed by their husbands or boyfriends.[85] In a study in the United States, murder was the second leading cause of death for girls aged 15 to 18, and 78 per cent of homicide victims in the study were killed by an acquaintance or an intimate partner.[86] In Colombia, every six days a woman is reportedly killed by her partner or former partner.[87]

A review of studies on intimate partner violence during pregnancy undertaken between 1963 and 1995 found that prevalence ranged from 0.9 per cent to 20.1 per cent of all pregnant women in the United States.[88] A 1996 study in Nicaragua found that 31 per cent of battered women reported having been subjected to physical violence during pregnancy.[89] Several studies across different developing countries indicate that violence during pregnancy ranges from 4 to 32 per cent, and that the prevalence of moderate to severe physical violence during pregnancy is about 13 per cent.[90]

Psychological or emotional violence against women has received less attention in research on intimate partner violence. Measuring such forms of violence is more difficult as specific behaviours vary significantly across different settings. There is no common understanding of which acts or combination of acts, and with what frequency, constitute emotional violence. The WHO multi-country study on domestic violence found that between 20 per cent and 75 per cent of women had experienced one or more emotionally abusive acts.[91] A multi-country population-based cross-sectional study conducted in Chile, Egypt, India and the Philippines found that the lifetime prevalence of severe psychological violence ranged from 10.5 per cent in Egypt to 50.7 per cent in Chile.[92] The first French national survey on violence against women found that 35 per cent of women had experienced psychological pressure by an intimate partner over a 12-month period. The definition of such pressure included attempts to control the other person's activities, imposing authority, or attitudes of denigration or contempt. Four per cent had experienced emotional blackmail or verbal abuse including insults and threats over the same period.[93] In a study in Germany, 42 per cent of respondents reported having experienced acts such as intimidation and aggressive yelling, slander, threats, humiliation and "psycho-terror".[94]

Harmful traditional practices

Female infanticide and prenatal sex selection, early marriage, dowry-related violence, female genital mutilation/cutting, crimes against women committed in the name of "honour", and maltreatment of widows, including inciting widows to commit suicide, are forms of violence against women that are considered harmful traditional practices, and may involve both family and community. While data has been gathered on some of these forms, this is not a comprehensive list of such practices. Others have been highlighted by States (for example in their reports to human rights treaty bodies and in follow-up reports on implementation of the Beijing Platform for Action), by the Special Rapporteur on violence against women, its causes and consequences and by the Special Rapporteur on harmful traditional practices.[95] They include the dedication of young girls to temples, restrictions on a second daughter's right to marry, dietary restrictions for pregnant women, forced feeding and nutritional taboos, marriage to a deceased husband's brother and witch hunts.[96]

The most extensive body of research concerns female genital mutilation/cutting. It is estimated that more than 130 million girls and women alive today have undergone female genital mutilation/cutting, mainly in Africa and some countries in the Middle East. The practice is also prevalent among immigrant communities in Europe, North America and Australia.[97] Surveys revealed significant geographic variations in the prevalence rates in 19 countries: 99 per cent in Guinea, 97 per cent in Egypt, 80 per cent in Ethiopia, 17 per cent in Benin, and 5 per cent in Ghana and Niger.[98] They also show that the practice may be slowly declining even in high prevalence countries because of increasing opposition from women's groups. Higher female educational levels, female access to and control over economic resources, ethnicity and women's own female genital mutilation/cutting status have been found to be significantly associated with their support for or opposition to female genital mutilation/cutting.[99]

Practices of son preference, expressed in manifestations such as female infanticide, prenatal sex selection and systematic neglect of girls, have resulted in adverse female-male sex ratios and high rates of female infant mortality in South and East Asia, North Africa, and the Middle East.[100] A study in India estimated that prenatal sex selection and infanticide have accounted for half a million missing girls per year for the past two decades.[101] In the Republic of Korea, among pregnancies having sex-identification tests, more than 90 per cent of pregnancies with male foetuses resulted in normal births, whereas more than 30 per cent of those with female foetuses were terminated, according to the National Fertility and Family Health Survey.[102]

Early marriages involve the marriage of a child, i.e. a person below the age of 18.[103] Minor girls have not achieved full maturity and capacity to act and lack ability to control their sexuality. When they marry and have children, their health can be adversely affected, their education impeded and economic autonomy restricted.[104] Early marriage also increases the risk of HIV infection.[105] Such marriages take place all over the world, but are most common in sub-Saharan Africa and South Asia, where more than 30 per cent of girls aged 15 to 19 are married.[106] In Ethiopia, it was found that 19 per cent of girls were married by the age of 15 and in some regions such as Amhara, the proportion was as high as 50 per cent.[107] In Nepal, 7 per cent of girls were married before the age of 10 and 40 per cent by the age of 15.[108] A UNICEF global assessment found that in Latin America and the Caribbean, 29 per cent of women aged 15 to 24 were married before the age of 18.[109]

A forced marriage is one lacking the free and valid consent of at least one of the parties.[110] In its most extreme form, forced marriage can involve threatening behaviour, abduction, imprisonment, physical violence, rape and, in some cases, murder. There has been little research on this form of violence. A recent European study confirmed the lack of quantitative surveys in Council of Europe countries.[111] One study of 1,322 marriages across six villages in Kyrgyzstan found that one half of ethnic Kyrgyz marriages were the result of kidnappings, and that as many as two thirds of these marriages were non-consensual.[112] In the United Kingdom, a Forced Marriage Unit established by the Government intervenes in 300 cases of forced marriage a year.[113]

Violence related to demands for dowry—which is the payment of cash or goods by the bride's family to the groom's family—may lead to women being killed in dowry-related femicide. According to official crime statistics in India, approximately 6,822 women were killed in 2002 as a result of such violence.[114] Small community studies have also indicated that dowry demands have played an important role in women being burned to death and in deaths of women labelled as suicides.[115]

Crimes against women committed in the name of "honour" may occur within the family or within the community. These crimes are receiving increased attention, but remain underreported and under-documented. The most severe manifestation is murder—so-called "honour killings". UNFPA estimated that 5,000 women are murdered by family members each year in "honour killings" around the world.[116] A government report noted that "karo-kari" ("honour killings") claimed the lives of 4,000 men and women between 1998 and 2003 in Pakistan, and that the number of women killed was more than double the number of men.[117]

Older women, including in particular widows, are subject to harmful practices in a number of countries, which can involve both the family and the community. A study conducted in Ghana, based on data collected from news reports and interviews, found that many poor, often elderly women were accused of witchcraft. Some were murdered by male relatives and those who survived were subjected to a range of physical, sexual and economic abuses.[118] Violence directed against widows, including sexual abuse and harassment and property-related violence at the hands of relatives, mainly in-laws, has been reported from a number of countries including India,[119] but information remains scarce.

Violence against women in the community

Women also face pervasive violence within the general community. Physical, sexual and psychological violence can be a daily feature of women's interactions in their neighbourhoods, on public transport, in workplaces, schools, sports clubs, colleges and hospitals, and in religious and other social institutions. Forms of violence against women and girls in the general community include femicide; sexual violence including rape; sexual harassment; trafficking in women and forced prostitution. This section focuses on femicide, sexual violence by non-partners, sexual harassment and trafficking in women.

Femicide: the gender-based murder of a woman

Femicide occurs everywhere, but the scale of some cases of femicide within community contexts—for example, in Ciudad Juárez, Mexico and Guatemala—has drawn attention to this aspect of violence against women. Most official sources agree that more than 320 women have been murdered in Ciudad Juárez, one third of whom were brutally raped.[120] In Guatemala, according to National Civil Police statistics, 1,467 women were murdered between 2001 and the beginning of December 2004.[121] Other sources claim the figure is higher, with 2,070 women murdered, mostly aged 14 to 35.[122] The killings have been concentrated in areas where the economies are dominated by *maquilas*, assembly plants for export products owned and operated in tax-free zones by multinational companies. Impunity for these crimes is seen as a key factor in these occurrences, and in the case of Guatemala, the legacy of the internal armed conflict that ended in 1996 is also seen as a contributing factor.[123]

Sexual violence by non-partners

Despite women being more at risk of violence from their intimate partners than from other people, sexual violence by non-partners is common in many settings. Sexual violence by non-partners refers to violence by a relative, friend, acquaintance, neighbour, work colleague or stranger. Estimates of the prevalence of sexual violence by non-partners are difficult to establish, because in many societies, sexual violence remains an issue of deep shame for women and often for their families. Statistics on rape extracted from police records, for example, are notoriously unreliable because of significant underreporting.

A number of population-based surveys have addressed the question of sexual violence by non-partners. The WHO multi-country study on domestic violence showed that the proportion of women who had suffered sexual violence by non partners after the age of 15 varied from less than 1 per cent in Ethiopia and Bangladesh to between 10 and 12 per cent in Peru, Samoa and the United Republic of Tanzania.[124] These findings are similar to those emerging from other population-based studies. In Canada, for example, 11.6 per cent of women reported sexual violence by a non-partner in their lifetime.[125] In New Zealand and Australia, studies have shown that between 10 and 20 per cent of women have experienced various forms of sexual violence from non-partners, including unwanted sexual touching, attempted rape and rape.[126] Preliminary results from Switzerland show that 22.3 per cent of women experience sexual violence by non-partners in their lifetime.[127]

Forced sexual initiation constitutes a significant sub-field of violence perpetrated by non-partners, but may also occur in the context of an intimate relationship. The 2002 WHO World Report on Violence and Health identified population-based surveys from six countries addressing the issue of forced sexual initiation. The figures range from 9 per cent in the United States to 40 per cent in Peru. Across all countries, three to four times more girls than boys reported forced sexual initiation.[128]

Dating violence is another form of sexual violence by non-partners experienced by young women. In Canada, for example, a study of adolescents aged 15 to 19 found that 54 per cent of girls had experienced "sexual coercion" in a dating relationship.[129] Findings from the United States in 2000 showed that the average prevalence of dating violence was 22 per cent for high-school students and 32 per cent for college students.[130] Research in the United States also found that 8.3 per cent of women had experienced physical aggression, rape, or stalking by a dating partner and 20.6 per cent of women reported more than one type of dating violence.[131] Young girls may be coerced into sexual relationships with older men who provide food, school fees or gifts in exchange for sex. These so-called "sugar daddies" place girls at risk of contracting HIV. In parts of Africa and Asia, the rape of young girls is linked to the myth that sex with a virgin will cure HIV.[132]

Sexual harassment and violence in the workplace, educational institutions and in sport

The phenomenon of harassment and violence in the workplace is receiving increasing attention, especially in the context of women's rising rates of participation in the labour force and enhanced legal and regulatory provisions. European surveys have shown significant rates of sexual harassment in the workplace, with between 40 and 50 per cent of women in the European Union reporting some form of sexual harassment or unwanted sexual behaviour in the workplace.[133] Small surveys in Asia-Pacific countries indicate that 30 to 40 per cent of women workers report some form of harassment—verbal, physical or sexual.[134]

Sexual harassment and violence against girls and young women in educational institutions is also the subject of increased research. Studies show that the extent of violence in schools may be significant. A study in the United States found that 83 per cent of girls in grades 8 through 11 in public schools experienced some form of sexual harassment.[135] A 2002 World Bank study found that 22 per cent of adolescent girls reported being victims of sexual abuse in educational settings in Ecuador.[136] According to a 2006 study of schoolgirls in Malawi, 50 per cent of the girls said they had been touched in a sexual manner "without permission, by either their teachers or fellow schoolboys".[137]

Women and girls who engage in sport may face the risk of gender-based violence, exploitation and harassment, from other athletes, spectators, coaches, managers and family or community members. A study indicated that 40 to 50 per cent of female athletes surveyed in Canada and 27 per cent in Australia, and 25 per cent of sportswomen under the age of 18 in Denmark reported harassment or knowing someone close to them that had been harassed.[138] Research in the Czech Republic found that 45 per cent of female athletes had experienced sexual harassment from someone in sport, with 27 per cent reporting harassment from a coach.[139]

Trafficking in women

Trafficking is a form of violence against women that takes place in multiple settings and usually involves many different actors including families, local brokers, international criminal networks and immigration authorities. Trafficking in human beings takes place both between and within countries. The majority of the victims of human trafficking are women and children, and many are trafficked for purposes of sexual exploitation.

A definition of trafficking is provided by the Protocol to Prevent, Suppress and Punish Trafficking in Persons, Especially Women and Children, supplementing the United Nations Convention against Transnational Organized Crime: "*Trafficking in persons* shall mean the recruitment, transportation, transfer, harbouring or receipt of persons by means of the threat or use of force or other forms of coercion, of abduction, of fraud, of deception, of the abuse of power or of a position of vulnerability or of the giving or receiving of payments or benefits to achieve the consent of a person having control over another person, for the purpose of exploitation. Exploitation shall include, at a minimum, the exploitation of prostitution of others or other forms of sexual exploitation, forced labour or services, slavery or practices similar to slavery, servitude, or the removal of organs".[140]

Measuring the extent of trafficking is difficult (*see sect. V*). Until recently, interpretations of what constitutes trafficking and how it should be measured differed widely, but the adoption of the Trafficking Protocol has helped to overcome this challenge. Efforts are under way at the national, regional and international level to improve data collection on trafficking. According to the UNODC database on human trafficking trends, there are 127 countries of origin and 137 countries of destination for trafficking in human beings. Countries in Central and South-Eastern Europe, the Commonwealth of Independent States and Asia are the most frequently mentioned countries of origin, followed by West Africa, Latin America and the Caribbean. Countries within Western Europe, Asia and North America are the most commonly reported destinations.[141]

Although various sources suggest that hundreds of thousands of people are trafficked globally every year, few come to the attention of authorities. For instance, in 2005, 506 victims were identified in Portugal, 412 in Mexico and 243 in Turkey. The number of traffickers prosecuted and convicted is also remarkably low. For instance, in 2003, 24 people were prosecuted and only 8 convicted in Lithuania, 59 were prosecuted and 11 convicted in Ukraine and, in 2004, 59 people were prosecuted and 43 convicted in the United States.[142]

Violence against women perpetrated or condoned by the State

The State—either through its agents or public policy—can perpetrate physical, sexual and psychological violence against women. State agents include all people empowered to exercise elements of State authority—members of the legislative, executive and judicial branches, as well as law enforcement officials, social security officials, prison guards, officials in places of detention, immigration officials and military and security forces.

State agents may commit violence on the streets and in custodial settings, and include acts of sexual violence including rape, sexual harassment and molestation. Some such acts may constitute torture or cruel, inhuman or degrading treatment or punishment. A State may also perpetrate violence against women through its laws and policies. Examples of such laws and policies include those that criminalize women's consensual sexual behaviour as a means to control women; policies on forced sterilization, forced pregnancy and forced abortion; policies on protective custody of women that effectively imprisons them; and other laws and policies, including policies on virginity testing and sanctioning forced marriages, that fail to recognize women's autonomy and agency and legitimize male control over women. States may also condone violence against women through inadequate laws or through ineffective implementation of laws, effectively allowing perpetrators of violence against women impunity for their acts (*see sect. VI*). This section addresses custodial violence and forced sterilization in more detail as examples of violence against women perpetrated or condoned by the State.

Custodial violence against women

Custodial violence against women in police cells, prisons, social welfare institutions, immigration detention centres and other State institutions constitutes violence perpetrated by the State. Sexual violence, including rape, perpetrated against women in detention is considered a particularly egregious violation of the inherent dignity and the right to physical integrity of human beings and accordingly may constitute torture.[143] Other forms of violence against women in custody that have been documented by various sources include: inappropriate surveillance during showers or undressing; strip searches conducted by or in the presence of men; and verbal sexual harassment. The control wielded by correctional officers over women's daily lives may also result in violence through demands for sexual acts in exchange for privileges, goods or basic necessities.[144] Although instances of custodial violence against women are reported in countries all around the world,[145] there is little quantitative data to establish the prevalence of such violence across countries.

Forced sterilization

The use of sterilization to control the reproductive behaviour of the female population or a particular subgroup, constitutes violence against women. While there are no systematic quantitative studies, the practice of forced sterilization has been confirmed and condemned in regional and national courts. Cases of forced or coerced sterilizations of certain populations such as Roma women and girls in Europe[146] and indigenous women in the United States and Canada[147] have been reported.

Violence against women in armed conflict

During armed conflict, women experience all forms of physical, sexual and psychological violence perpetrated by both State and non-State actors. These forms include murder, unlawful killings, torture and other cruel, inhuman or degrading treatment or punishment, abductions, maiming and mutilation, forced recruitment of women combatants, rape, sexual slavery, sexual exploitation, involuntary disappearance, arbitrary detention, forced marriage, forced prostitution, forced abortion, forced pregnancy and forced sterilization.

Sexual violence has been used during armed conflict for many different reasons, including as a form of torture, to inflict injury, to extract information, to degrade and intimidate and to destroy communities. Rape of women has been used to humiliate opponents, to drive communities and groups off land and to wilfully spread HIV.[148] Women have been forced to perform sexual and domestic slave labour.[149] Women have also been abducted and then forced to serve as "wives" to reward fighters.[150]

The incidence of violence against women in armed conflict, particularly sexual violence including rape, has been increasingly acknowledged and documented.[151] Violence against women has been reported from conflict or post-conflict situations in many countries or areas.

Four population-based surveys on violence against women in contexts of armed conflict are outlined in table 1. It is estimated that between 250,000 and 500,000 women in Rwanda were raped during the 1994 genocide, that between 20,000 and 50,000 women were raped in Bosnia during the conflict in the early 1990s,[152] and around 200,000 women and girls were raped during the armed conflict in Bangladesh in 1971.[153]

Table 1
Sexual violence against women in conflict settings

Setting (period of conflict)	Type of research	Results[a]
Liberia (1989–1994)	Random survey of 205 women in Monrovia aged 15 to 79	49 per cent (100) women reported at least 1 act of violence by a combatant: 17 per cent reported being beaten, tied up or detained in a room under armed guard; 32 per cent were strip-searched once or more; 15 per cent reported being raped, subjected to attempted rape, or sexually coerced.
Uganda (1980–1986)	N/A, Luwero District, Northern Uganda	70 per cent of women in Luwero District reported being raped by soldiers. A large proportion had been gang-raped by groups of up to 10 soldiers.
Former East Timor (1999)	Population-based survey of 288 women	24 per cent of women reported a violent episode from someone outside the family during the 1999 conflict; of these, 96 per cent included improper sexual comments and 92 per cent being threatened with a weapon.
Sierra Leone (1991–1999)	Population-based survey of internally displaced women living in 3 camps and 1 town in 2001: 991 women provided information on 9,166 household members	13 per cent (1,157) of household members reported some form of war-related human rights abuses; 9 per cent of respondents and 8 per cent of female household members reported war-related sexual violence.

[a] For references, see note 229.

Ending violence against women: From words to action

Violence against women and multiple discrimination

Forms and manifestations of violence against women are shaped by social and cultural norms as well as the dynamics of each social, economic and political system. Factors such as women's race, ethnicity, caste, class, migrant or refugee status, age, religion, sexual orientation, marital status, disability or HIV status will influence what forms of violence they suffer and how they experience it.

In many societies, women belonging to particular ethnic or racial groups are likely to experience gender-based violence as well as violence based on their ethnic or racial identity.[154] Indigenous women are subject to various forms of violence, including intimate partner violence, custodial violence by police and murder, sometimes at a much higher rate than non-indigenous women.[155] According to a 1996 Canadian Government statistic, indigenous women in Canada between the ages of 25 and 44 were five times more likely than all other women of the same age to die as the result of violence.[156] In the United States, a 1999 study found that indigenous women were more than twice as likely as white women to be the victims of violent crime.[157] A 2003 study found that Australian indigenous women were 28 times more likely than non-indigenous women to be admitted to hospital with assault injuries.[158]

In India, violence against women based on caste is manifested in high rates of sexual violence committed against Dalit women by men of higher caste. In particularly remote villages, access to a Dalit woman's body is considered the prerogative of the landlord of the village.[159]

Older women, who form a large proportion of the world's growing elderly population, are subject to particular forms and manifestations of violence. Elder abuse usually refers to women over 60 or 65, but some studies include those over 50. Violence against older women may take the form of physical, sexual or psychological abuse, as well as financial exploitation or neglect, which can be perpetrated by family members or other caregivers.

Women may encounter violence based on social prejudices against them because of their sexual orientation. Forms of violence against lesbian women because of their sexual orientation include non-partner sexual violence, sexual enslavement, forced marriage and murder. In the United States, for example, lesbian women may be targeted for acts of violence in prisons, by the police and by members of their family and community. Numerous cases document lesbians being beaten, raped, forcibly impregnated or married against their will.[160] There have also been cases of lesbians being incarcerated for gender identity disorders in mental hospitals by family or community members.[161]

Women with disabilities may experience violence in particular ways in their homes and institutional settings, perpetrated by family members, caretakers or strangers. Surveys conducted in Europe, North America and Australia have shown that over half of women with disabilities have experienced physical abuse, compared to one third of non-disabled women.[162]

About 90 million women currently reside outside their countries of origin, about half of the world's international migrants.[163] Because of their subordinate status both as migrants and as women, female migrant workers are highly vulnerable to exploitation and ill-treatment.[164] The types of violence suffered by women migrant workers include: inhumane working conditions, such as long working hours, non-payment of wages and forced confinement; starvation; beatings; rape; and being forced into prostitution. Unskilled workers, particularly in domestic service, experience greater and different kinds of violence than other women.[165] Migrant women may also experience intimate partner violence and their status as migrants may further curtail their access to escape routes, services and information.[166]

Of the 10.9 million persons of concern to UNHCR, roughly half are female (49 per cent).[167] Stripped of the protection of their homes, their Government and often their family structure, refugee and displaced women may be subject to different forms of violence, abuse and exploitation, including rape and abduction, during flight, in refugee camps as well as in asylum countries. Perpetrators of such violence may include military personnel, border guards, resistance units, male refugees and others with whom they come in contact.

Areas requiring enhanced attention

While all forms and manifestations of violence against women require more attention, some have been especially neglected. Psychological and emotional abuse and violence can take different forms that need to be made more visible and explicitly addressed. In this regard, acts such as incarceration of women in mental hospitals or in prisons for not conforming to social and cultural expectations, restrictions placed on women, such as locking them up or enforcing their isolation and limiting interaction with others, have been documented anecdotally but remain largely invisible. Knowledge about violence against women in institutional settings, including in schools, hospitals, prisons and different detention facilities also remains very limited. Economic abuse and exploitation, including acts such as withholding of income, forcibly usurping women's wages and denying basic necessities, are manifestations that require greater visibility and attention, especially in the context of growing female participation in the labour force around the world. The abuse of older women may become more prevalent with changing demographics. While femicide is gaining recognition, the underlying dynamic of gender inequality that fuels the murders of women in different contexts is still inadequately understood. More inquiry is also needed about the use of technology, such as computers and cell phones, in developing and expanding forms of violence. Evolving and emerging forms of violence need to be named so that they can be recognized and better addressed.

Consequences of violence against women

Violence against women is a violation of women's human rights and prevents women from enjoying their human rights and fundamental freedoms, such as the rights to life and security of the person, to the highest attainable standard of physical and mental health, to education, work and housing and to participation in public life. Such violence perpetuates the subordination of women and the unequal distribution of power between women and men. It has consequences for women's health and well-being, carries a heavy human and economic cost, hinders development and can also lead to displacement.

Health consequences

Violence places women at higher risk for poor physical and reproductive health.[168] Abused women also show poorer mental health and social functioning.[169] Women subjected to violence are more likely to abuse alcohol and drugs and to report sexual dysfunction, suicide attempts, post-traumatic stress and central nervous system disorders.[170]

Violence against women frequently leads to death. Femicide, suicide, AIDS-related deaths and maternal mortality can be fatal consequences of violence against women. There is little data on lethal outcomes of violence against women, such as the proportions of maternal deaths and AIDS mortality directly attributable to the different forms of violence women suffer. A few studies based in health facilities indicate a relationship between intimate partner violence and death during pregnancy. For example, a study of 400 villages and seven hospitals in rural western India found that 16 per cent of all deaths during pregnancy were the result of partner violence.[171] A similar trend has been found in Bangladesh and the United States.[172]

There are extensive physical health consequences of violence against women. These include physical injuries, such as fractures and abdominal/thoracic injuries, and chronic health conditions, including chronic pain and gastrointestinal disorders. Reproductive health consequences include gynaecological disorders, pelvic inflammatory disease, sexually transmitted infections, including HIV, unwanted pregnancies and poor obstetric outcomes.[173] Other gynaecological consequences include vaginal bleeding or infection, chronic pelvic pain and urinary tract infections. A study in the United States, for example, found that the prevalence of women with gynaecological problems among victims of spousal abuse was three times higher than the average.[174]

For many women worldwide, the threat of violence exacerbates their risk of contracting HIV. Fear of violence prevents women from accessing HIV/AIDS information, being tested, disclosing their HIV status, accessing services for the prevention of HIV transmission to infants and receiving treatment and counselling, even when they know they have been infected. Studies show the increasing links between violence against women and HIV and demonstrate that HIV-infected women are more likely to have experienced violence, and that women who have experienced violence are at higher risk for HIV.[175]

Unintended pregnancy is another important consequence of sexual violence. Rape increases the risk of unintended pregnancy. In the context of armed conflict, for example in Bosnia and Herzegovina, and Rwanda, women have been raped repeatedly until they conceived, as part of a strategy of ethnic cleansing.[176] A woman's fear of violence from her husband or partner may make her afraid to bring up the issue of contraceptive use, leading to unintended pregnancy. A study of women in Colombia, for example, found that women who experienced intimate partner violence had higher rates of unintended pregnancy.[177] Unintended pregnancy has serious repercussions—unsafe abortions, suicides and family reactions that can include social isolation, ostracism or even murder.

Violence before and during pregnancy has serious health consequences for both mother and child. Violence leads to high-risk pregnancies and a range of pregnancy-related problems including miscarriage, preterm labour, foetal distress and low birth weight.[178] A 2002 study in Nicaragua, for example, found that 16 per cent of the low birth weight in the infant population could be attributed to physical abuse by a partner during pregnancy.[179]

Violence against women can result in both physical injury and harm to a woman's reproductive health. For trafficked women, the most common health consequences include chronic pain, malnutrition and unhealthy weight loss. Trafficked women also may suffer from sexually transmitted infections, permanent damage to the reproductive organs, and psychological damage from domination and isolation.[180] Female genital mutilation/cutting is itself a form of physical trauma that can lead to severe pain, shock, haemorrhaging, infection and ulceration of the genital area. Haemorrhage and infection can lead to death. The long-term consequences can include abscesses, dermoid cysts and keloid scars, obstructed labour resulting in increased risk of maternal and child morbidity and mortality, infertility and lasting psychological effects.[181] Female genital mutilation/cutting also places women at a higher risk of HIV infection.

The psychological consequences of violence against women can be as grave as the physical effects. Depression is one of the most common consequences of sexual and physical violence against women.

Women who suffer from violence are also at a higher risk of stress and anxiety disorders, including post-traumatic stress disorder.[182] A study in Michigan, United States, for example, found that 59 per cent of women who had experienced severe abuse in the previous 12 months had psychological problems, compared to 20 per cent of those who reported no abuse.[183] Studies have shown that rape, childhood sexual abuse, and intimate partner violence are the most common causes of post-traumatic stress disorder in women. Experts have also identified the "traumatic syndrome of abused women", which includes lack of volitional autonomy, fear, anguish, depression and, in some cases, suicide.[184]

Depression and attempted suicide are closely associated with intimate partner violence. It has also been shown that girls who have been raped or experienced sexual harassment are at increased risk of suicide.[185] Post-traumatic stress disorder, in particular, appears to be a significant risk factor for suicide.[186]

Social and intergenerational impacts

Violence against women prevents women from fully participating in their communities socially or economically. Women who are targeted for violence are less likely to be employed, tend to be employed in low status jobs and are unlikely to be promoted.[187] Sexual violence undermines physical security in public areas and the risk of such violence may increase when women enter public life, constraining their political voice.[188] For example, in Sri Lanka, the continuing conflict has created a culture of violence against women that has limited their political participation.[189] One study in Mexico found that women often stopped participating in community development projects because of threats from men.[190]

The societal consequences of trafficking in women include the separation of children from their families; loss of education; stigmatization of the women, who therefore require long-term social support; and the growth of criminal activities.[191]

Research indicates that violence against women in the family and social violence are closely linked.[192] Witnessing chronic domestic violence can be the start of a lifelong pattern of delinquency and the use of violence in personal relationships.[193]

Children are often present during episodes of domestic violence and those who witness it may suffer a range of behavioural and emotional problems. Research suggests that violence in the family affects children in at least three main ways: their health; their educational performance; and their use of violence in their own lives.[194] Children who witness violence may exhibit more fearful and antisocial behaviour. They also have been found to show more anxiety, depression, trauma symptoms and temperament problems than other children.[195] These children also tend to exhibit more aggressive behaviour towards their peers.[196] Exposure to chronic violence is associated with lower cognitive functioning and poor school performance.[197] A study in Nicaragua found that children of female victims of violence left school an average of four years earlier than other children.[198] At the same time, most children who witness violence at home will not become violent and these different reactions need to be better understood. However, children who do exhibit violent behaviour are more likely to continue that behaviour and transmit it to future generations.[199]

Domestic or intimate partner violence against women can also be fatal for children. A Nicaraguan study found that children of women who were physically abused by a partner were six times more likely than other children to die before the age of five.[200]

Economic costs of violence against women

Violence against women impoverishes individual women and their families, as well as their communities, societies and nations at many levels. It reduces the capacity of victims/survivors to contribute productively to the family, the economy and public life; drains resources from social services, the justice system, health-care agencies and employers; and lowers the overall educational attainment, mobility and innovative potential of the victims/survivors, their children and even the perpetrators of such violence.[201]

Analysing the costs of violence against women is useful for understanding the severity of the problem as it shows its economic impact on businesses, the State, community groups and individuals. It emphasizes the pervasiveness of such violence and confirms that it is a public concern, not a private issue. Such analysis can provide important information for specific budgetary allocations for programmes to prevent and redress violence against women and demonstrates that much more should be invested in early intervention and prevention strategies, rather than allowing such violence to continue unabated.

There are several types of costs, in the short and long term: first, the direct cost of services in relation to violence against women; second, the indirect cost of lost employment and productivity; and third, the value placed on human pain and suffering.

The direct cost of services in relation to violence against women include the actual expenditure by individuals, Governments and businesses on goods, facilities and services to treat and support victims/survivors and to bring perpetrators to justice. Services include the criminal justice system (such as for the police, prosecution, courts, prisons, offender programmes, the administration of community sentences and victim compensation); health services (such as for primary and hospital health care for both physical and mental harm); housing (such as shelters, refuges and re-housing); social services (especially in relation to the care of children); income support; other support services (such as rape crisis counselling, telephone advice lines); and civil legal costs (such as those for legal injunctions to remove violent men from the home or otherwise restrain them and for legal separation and divorce proceedings).

The cost of these services is mostly borne by the State/public sector. While the criminal justice system is almost universally funded by the State, the funding for other services varies. In some countries, support services and refuges are primarily provided by volunteers or the community sector, while in others such services are provided by the public sector either directly or through State funding for service providers. In some countries, health care is provided by the public sector, while in others, individuals carry the costs directly or through private insurance.

The second major category of costs relates to reduced employment and productivity, a category sometimes described as the cost to the private or business sector. Women may be absent from employment as a result of injury or trauma, or may work at a level of reduced productivity because of injuries and stress. Further costs arise when women lose jobs either as a result of absence and reduced performance, or because they have been compelled to relocate. Both workers and employers face costs as a result of such disruption to employment. While women may lose earnings, employers may lose output and may face the costs of sick leave and of recruiting and training replacements. Some studies include the lost revenue to the State in taxation as a consequence of lost employment and output.

The third category of cost is that of the value placed on the pain and suffering inflicted on women. This is an intangible cost borne by the victim/survivor. Increasingly, government cost-benefit analyses include the value of "pain and suffering" in a range of areas. For example, they include such costs in their calculations of the impact of crime or when they assess the costs of road traffic accidents when planning new roads.

There are other costs that are imposed by violence against women, but which are very difficult to estimate. Some studies note them as a category, but do not include a figure in the estimates. One important such cost is that of the consequences for children who witness violence, such as their need for counselling, given the psychological damage they endure, and the long-term costs of lower levels of educational and employment achievement.

While some studies on the cost of violence against women focus on specific types of cost, the majority include both the cost of services and lost earnings. Some more recent studies additionally include the cost of pain and suffering. The first study on the economic costs of violence against women was conducted in Australia in 1988. Most of the studies have been conducted in developed countries. New research, as yet unpublished, is being carried out in Bulgaria, Fiji, South Africa and Uganda. Since 1994, the World Bank has noted the cost of domestic violence.[202] The main studies, including the costs calculated, are summarized in annex 2.

The costs calculated in these studies vary considerably as a result of differences in methodology. In Canada, the annual costs of direct expenditures related to violence against women were estimated at 684 million Canadian dollars for the criminal justice system, 187 million for police and 294 million for the cost of counselling and training, totalling more than 1 billion a year.[203] In the United Kingdom, the study examined the cost categories of justice, health care, social services, housing, legal, lost output and pain and suffering and estimated the resulting cost of domestic violence to be 23 billion pounds sterling (£) per year or £440 per person.[204] A 1998 national random survey of 7,000 Finnish women on rates and consequences of violence was later used to estimate the economic costs of violence against women in Finland.[205] The study measured the direct costs of health care, social services, police, courts and incarceration and also the indirect costs of the value of lost lives and time lost from paid work and volunteer labour. The annual cost was estimated at 101 million euros (€) per year, or approximately €20 per person. A World Bank study estimated that domestic violence and rape account for 5 per cent of the total disease burden for women aged 15 to 44 in developing countries and 19 per cent in developed countries.[206]

The costs of violence against women are enormous. They impoverish not only individuals, families, communities and Governments, but also reduce the economic development of each nation. Even the most comprehensive surveys to date underestimate the costs, given the number of factors not included. Nonetheless, they all show that the failure to address violence against women has serious economic consequences, highlighting the need for determined and sustained preventive action.■

V. COLLECTING DATA ON VIOLENCE AGAINST WOMEN

Introduction

The number of studies conducted to estimate the prevalence of different forms of violence against women, particularly intimate partner violence, expanded greatly in the second half of the 1990s. According to a 2006 United Nations report, at least one survey on violence against women had been conducted in 71 countries and at least one national survey was available in 41 countries.[207]

Studies on violence against women have been carried out by a wide variety of bodies, including government ministries, national statistical offices, universities, international agencies, NGOs and women's rights organizations. The results have provided compelling evidence that violence against women is a severe and pervasive human rights violation throughout the world, with devastating effects on the health and well-being of women and children.

Despite the progress in recent years, however, there is still an urgent need to strengthen the knowledge base on all forms of violence against women to inform policy and strategy development. Many countries still lack reliable data and much of the existing information cannot be meaningfully compared. Moreover, very few countries collect data on violence against women on a regular basis, which would allow changes over time to be measured. More data are urgently needed on how various forms of violence against women affect different groups of women, requiring that data be disaggregated according to factors such as age and ethnicity. Little information is available to assess the measures taken to combat violence against women and to evaluate their impact.

Both policymakers and activists have called for the development of a comprehensive set of international indicators on violence against women.[208] These international indicators would need to be based on widely available and credible data collected at the national level, using comparable methods to define and measure violence.

More and better quality data are needed to guide national policies and programmes and to monitor States' progress in addressing violence. Ensuring an adequate knowledge base through data collection is part of every State's obligation to address violence against women. States should take responsibility for the systematic collection and publication of data under the framework of official statistics, including supporting NGOs, academics and others engaged in such work. State responsibility and accountability for addressing, preventing and eliminating violence against women is, however, not reduced because data is inadequate or unavailable.

Population-based surveys

Description of population-based surveys

Population-based or household surveys that ask women about their experiences of violence are considered the most reliable method for obtaining information on violence against women in a general population. Population-based surveys use randomly selected samples and their results are therefore representative of the larger population. Because they include the experiences of women regardless of whether they have reported the violence to authorities or not, population-based surveys are likely to give a more accurate picture than data from administrative records. This makes them particularly useful for measuring the extent of violence against women, monitoring trends over time, building awareness and developing policy. When studies performed in different countries use similar methods to measure violence, it is also possible to compare the risk of violence that women face and understand the similarities and differences between settings.

There are two major approaches to collecting population-based data on violence against women. The first involves "dedicated" surveys specifically designed to gather detailed information on different forms of violence against women. The second includes questions or modules on violence against women within large-scale surveys designed to generate information on broader issues such as poverty, crime or reproductive health.

The Violence against Women Survey, carried out by Statistics Canada in 1993, was one of the first national dedicated surveys. Similar national surveys have since been carried out in other countries, including Australia,[209] Finland,[210] France,[211] Germany,[212] New Zealand,[213] Sweden[214] and the United States.[215]

The methodology of these surveys has been further refined. The WHO has developed a comprehensive research methodology, reflected in its multi-country study on domestic violence, which has been implemented in at least 12 mainly resource-poor countries (*see box 6*). A standardized instrument for international surveys on violence against women has also been developed and implemented in 11 (mostly developed) countries to date (*see box 6*).[216] The development of research instruments that have been validated and used in a wide variety of settings has greatly increased the capacity of countries to produce reliable, credible and comparable data on violence against women. However, standard methodology for the implementation of surveys on violence against women within the framework of official statistics has not yet been developed at the international or supranational level.[217]

In addition to measuring the prevalence of different forms of violence against women, such dedicated surveys gather detailed information on a broad range of violence and its causes, as well as some information on perpetrators. Some also record the circumstances and consequences of violence and women's responses and use of services. Dedicated surveys tend to devote more attention to training than general surveys and address issues of safety and confidentiality more comprehensively. Experience to date indicates that prevalence estimates from dedicated surveys tend to be higher than those from general surveys. The main disadvantage of dedicated studies is their cost, which may pose challenges for repeating them on a regular basis.

The second approach to data collection—integrating special modules on violence against women into general surveys—is particularly useful when resources are scarce. Questions or modules on violence against women have been included in demographic and health surveys and in reproductive health surveys in a number of countries, including in Cambodia, Colombia, the Dominican Republic, Egypt, Haiti, India, Nicaragua, Peru and Zambia.[218] Several Governments routinely conduct population-based crime surveys that include information on violence against women. For example, in the United States, the National Crime Victimization Survey (formerly known as the National Crime Survey) has been conducted since the 1960s, while in the United Kingdom, the British Crime Survey has been carried out since 1982. Statistics Canada has adapted a module of questions from the 1993 Violence against Women Survey and included it in the ongoing General Social Survey on Victimization, which is conducted at regular five-year intervals.

Box 6
Multi-country surveys on violence against women

The WHO multi-country study on women's health and domestic violence against women has been conducted in at least 12 countries and has involved over 24,000 women. The study collects data on women's experiences of intimate partner violence, sexual assault and child sexual abuse. The WHO study also collects data on a broad range of negative health outcomes commonly associated with violence, on risk and protective factors for intimate partner violence and on strategies and services that women use to deal with this violence.[a]

The International Violence against Women Survey has been carried out in 11 countries to date. The survey collects data from a nationally representative sample on a broad range of violent acts perpetrated by men against women, including physical and sexual violence. It is conducted within a crime victimization framework and provides information that is particularly useful for interventions in the criminal justice sector.[b]

---

[a] WHO Multi-Country Study on Women's Health and Domestic Violence against Women and Initial Results on Prevalence, Health Outcomes and Women's Responses (Geneva, WHO, 2005).

[b] Nevala, S., The International Violence against Women Surveys (Geneva, European Institute for Crime Prevention and Control, 2005).

An advantage of general surveys is that the broad variety of information collected in these surveys, such as reproductive and child health outcomes, can deepen understanding of the risk factors and health and other consequences of violence against women. Their regularity can allow monitoring over time of violence against women and its intergenerational consequences. However, the number of questions that can be included in a general survey is usually limited. Moreover, as there is less opportunity to develop rapport with the respondents, women may be less likely to report violence in these surveys.

Both dedicated surveys and general surveys can contribute valuable data for guiding interventions on violence against women and States should be encouraged to use the approach that best serves their needs and capacities.

Gaps and challenges in population-based data on violence against women

Despite recent multi-country initiatives, more work is needed to ensure greater uniformity and comparability in the collection and reporting of data on all forms of violence against women. For example, many of the prevalence estimates for intimate partner violence are not comparable because of methodological differences in the way that violence has been defined and measured. Moreover, there are enormous gaps in terms of geographic coverage, population groups addressed and types of violence measured.

Types of violence measured

Population-based surveys have examined many different types of violence against women, including intimate partner violence, sexual violence, female genital mutilation/cutting, child sexual abuse and emotional abuse. The majority of studies focus on just one type of violence, most commonly intimate partner violence or sexual violence. Studies on intimate partner violence usually address physical, sexual and emotional/psychological violence. Some studies also measure controlling behaviours on the part of the husband and economic abuse, such as denying a woman access or control over resources including her own income, as well as attitudes towards violence, such as the circumstances under which a husband is perceived as being justified in hitting his wife.

There has been significant progress in documenting the extent of female genital mutilation/cutting through the addition of a special module on female gential mutilation/cutting in demographic and health surveys and in surveys carried out by UNICEF. To date, these surveys have collected data on female genital mutilation/cutting in more than 20 countries.[219] They include information on the prevalence of female gential mutilation/cutting at national and regional levels, types of female gential mutilation/cutting performed, who performed the procedure and opinions about whether the practice should be continued.

However, other forms of violence identified in the Beijing Platform for Action have not been documented to the same extent (*see below, p. 78*). Because many of these forms of violence occur less frequently, or in specific populations, they are difficult to study using population-based surveys, and are best addressed through other methods.

Box 7
Prevalence and incidence[a]

The prevalence of violence against women refers to the proportion of "at-risk" women in a population who have experienced violence. For some kinds of violence, such as sexual violence, all women may be considered to be "at risk". For others, such as intimate partner violence, only women who have or have had an intimate partner would be considered at risk. Prevalence estimates usually present the percentage of women who have experienced violence either during the previous 12 months (known as point prevalence) or at any time in their life (lifetime prevalence).

The incidence rate refers to the number of acts of violence women experience during a specific period, such as one year, rather than the number of women who have been targeted. In crime studies, incidence of violence is generally measured as the number of assaults per inhabitant.

_____

[a] Ellsberg, M. and Heise, L., *Researching violence against women: a practical guide for researchers and activists* (Washington D.C., WHO, PATH, 2005).

Ethical and safety issues

Despite the sensitivity of the topic, it is possible to collect reliable and valid information on violence against women. However, specific safeguards are needed to protect both respondents and interviewers. WHO has developed safety and ethical guidelines for conducting research on domestic violence and on trafficking (*see boxes 4 and 8*). These address issues such as guaranteeing the safety of both respondents and interviewers; ensuring the privacy and confidentiality of the interview; providing special training on gender equality issues and violence against women to interviewers; providing a minimal level of information or referrals for respondents in situations of risk; and providing emotional and technical support for interviewers. Failure to adhere to these measures can compromise the quality of the data and put respondents and interviewers at risk of physical or emotional harm.

> **Box 8**
> **World Health Organization ethical and safety recommendations for research on domestic violence against women**
>
> a. The safety of respondents and the research team is paramount and should inform all project decisions.
>
> b. Prevalence studies need to be methodologically sound and build upon current research experience about how to minimize the underreporting of abuse.
>
> c. Protecting confidentiality is essential to ensure both women's safety and data quality.
>
> d. All research team members should be carefully selected and receive specialized training and ongoing support.
>
> e. The study design must include a number of actions aimed at reducing any possible distress caused to the participants by the research.
>
> f. Fieldworkers should be trained to refer women requesting assistance to available sources of support. Where few resources exist, it may be necessary for the study to create short-term support mechanisms.
>
> g. Researchers and donors have an ethical obligation to help ensure that their findings are properly interpreted and used to advance policy and intervention development.
>
> h. Violence questions should be incorporated into surveys designed for other purposes only when ethical and methodological requirements can be met.

Study design and implementation

The way that violence is defined and measured in population-based surveys varies a great deal. For example, some studies use definitions based on national criminal codes, while others allow respondents to define themselves as victims of violence. Further, while some surveys use a single direct question such as "Have you ever been beaten by anyone?", others use more specific multiple questions such as "Have you ever been slapped? or kicked? or beaten?" It has been shown that women are more likely to disclose violence if they are offered more than one opportunity to respond to a series of behaviourally specific questions; single questions to assess violence are not recommended. Studies that use only a few questions generally provide the lowest estimates of violence. Other issues, such as the way the surveys are administered and who is included in the study population, can also have a major influence on study results (*see box 8*).

Other sources of data and information on violence against women

Service-based data

Information that is collected routinely through public and private agencies that come into contact with women who have suffered violence is known as service-based data. It includes records from health centres, police stations and courts, public services such as housing and social welfare services and shelters and other support services for survivors of violence. Other support services include women lawyers' associations, legal aid services and advocacy organizations. Service-based data cannot be used to measure the prevalence of violence in a community since in most societies very few abused women report violence to the police or support services, and those who do tend to be the most seriously injured. However, service-based data can contribute to understanding sector responses to violence and how far they meet the needs of women.

Service-based data can be used to monitor the number of women coming forward to various agencies for help and can identify how many women have sought support due to violence in specific populations, for example, those attending health-care services. Information on the number of women utilizing particular services because of violence can provide estimates of the need for such services and their costs. It can also be used to quantify the need for training among service providers, including medical and criminal justice professionals.

Service-based data can also contribute to evaluating the response of agencies to which women turn for help. It is important to know, for example, how police respond when a woman reports violence. Is the case investigated, are arrests made and are the charges pursued through the courts? Data from police and courts are also needed to evaluate and formulate legislation, policies and procedures to respond to violence.

Box 9
Issues that affect the comparability of data on violence against women[a]

a. How is the study population identified?

   - What are the cut-off ages, for example over 18, between 15 and 49?

   - Are unmarried women excluded?

   - What geographic area is included in the study?

b. How is violence defined and measured?

   - Who defines the abuse—the researcher or the respondent?

   - Over what period of time is violence being measured?

   - Does the study distinguish between different types of perpetrators in terms of their relationship to the victim?

   - Is frequency of violence measured?

   - What types of violence are included (physical, sexual, emotional or economic)?

   - Does the study gather information regarding the severity of violence?

c. Is the interview carried out in such a way that women are likely to disclose experiences of violence?

   - How are questions on violence worded?

   - How are the questions introduced?

   - What questions precede them?

   - How many opportunities do the respondents have to disclose?

   - What is the context of the interview, in terms of privacy, length and skill of interviewer?

   - How is the interview administered, for example, face-to-face, by telephone or using computer technology?

[a] Ellsberg, M. and Heise, L., *Researching violence against women: a practical guide for researchers and activists* (Washington, D.C., WHO, PATH, 2005).

Tracking the availability of services, such as shelters or refuges and other support for women who have been subjected to violence is also needed to evaluate a society's response to the problem. In addition, this information provides important context to analyses of the numbers of women coming forward for help. For example, growth in the availability of services may explain growth in the numbers seeking help. At the same time, low numbers of women using shelters or other services should not be interpreted as low demand or need in areas where few such services exist. This instead may point to obstacles preventing women from seeking services.

Health services

Women who have been targeted for violence can be identified in a health-care setting where they seek treatment, care and support. However, women often do not disclose the fact that they have suffered violence, even when it is the underlying cause of their health-care visit. One way of increasing disclosure is through routine enquiry about violence. However, where routine enquiry takes place, the health service needs to have the capacity to respond appropriately and make referrals, as well as to record, analyse and report the data.

There is considerable debate about whether health workers who identify victims of violence should be obliged to report cases to the criminal justice system (mandatory reporting). Many health workers believe that this is a breach of privacy and confidentiality and can result in lower disclosure and increased risk for women. Health workers have also raised ethical concerns about routine identification of women who need help when the health-care system is unable to provide appropriate assistance.

Routine data collection of specific health outcomes related to violence, such as injury or death from homicide, offer potential for monitoring trends in violence against women, particularly intimate partner violence and sexual assault by partners and other perpetrators.

Criminal and civil justice sectors

Statistics may be collected more systematically in the criminal and civil justice sectors than in other sectors. The police are often the primary source of information on intimate partner homicides and other types of femicide. The criminal justice sector has the potential to collect information on both victims and perpetrators and to track repeat victimization and repeat offending. Because these sectors operate on the basis of a code of law, it should be possible to organize data by criminal code sections. In most countries, however, it is not possible to gain a complete picture of the magnitude of violence against women because statistics are not broken down according to the sex of the victim and do not describe the relationship of the victim to the perpetrator. Some countries have specific laws on domestic violence while others address domestic violence under laws on assault, grievous bodily harm, sexual assault, stalking, homicide and other crimes. Even within an individual country, different ministries may record the same crime differently, in light of different responsibilities, such as the ministry of justice and the ministry of health.

Although criminal court cases represent a very small and non-representative sample of cases of violence against women, court statistics are important. They can contribute to understanding the response of the criminal justice system to violence against women. In particular, the effectiveness of laws and sanctions designed to protect women can be assessed through statistics that track repeat offenders. However, in many countries, feedback from the courts to the ministry of justice is inadequate.

Women escaping domestic violence also use civil law remedies. In some countries civil injunctions, also known as protection orders, peace bonds, restraining orders or domestic violence orders, prohibit violent partners from coming into contact with the victim. They can include other conditions, such as prohibitions on the use of drugs or alcohol or on the possession of weapons. Other types of injunctions can remove the violent partner from the home. More data needs to be collected to ascertain how effective these measures are and how accessible they are to the women who need them.

Other services

Most public agencies that provide services to women victims/survivors of violence routinely keep some statistics on the use of their services. The quality and quantity of data collection varies considerably, both in general and in relation to violence against women. Such services include public agencies providing housing, child welfare and other social services.

Diverse support services, usually led by NGOs, sometimes with support from public funds, also collect information on the extent and nature of violence against the women who come to them for help. These services include shelters and refuges, advice telephone lines and advocacy and related support services. Information is also sometimes collected by women's lawyers' associations and legal aid services. The information collected by services such as these is particularly relevant to qualitative research. However, the records vary considerably in the type and quality of information collected.

Gaps and challenges in service-based data on violence against women

The availability and quality of service-based data varies a great deal. In some countries, particularly in Europe and North America, information is available, although not always compiled or disseminated, from a broad array of sources. In other countries, particularly those with limited resources, the obstacles to collecting service-based data on violence against women are much greater.

In general, service agencies do not have data collection as their primary responsibility and data available through these agencies are often not collected in a systematic way. The quality of the data may be poor, inconsistent over time and not entirely representative. Double counting is a common problem, whereby women seeking repeated services from the same agency or from more than one agency are counted more than once. These problems are largely the result of inadequate training, lack of resources and poor coordination among agencies.

Problems with service-based statistics are compounded when social services are sparse or non-existent or when violence against women is largely ignored by police or society in general. In societies where victims/survivors of domestic violence or sexual violence are highly stigmatized, they are reluctant to come forward for support. As a result, considerable variation exists in the extent to which service-based statistics are available at the national level. In order to improve data collection in this field, a parallel improvement in the number and quality of services for victims/survivors of violence is required, as well as a reduction in the stigma and discrimination they face.

Qualitative data collection

The main disadvantage of population-based surveys and service-based data is that the information they provide is often fairly limited—a survey may indicate how many women have experienced violence or how many have reported violence to the police, but may provide little or no information on how women experience violence, the cultural context of violence or the barriers that women face in access to justice. In contrast to quantitative research methods, which produce information that can be presented numerically, qualitative methods gather information that is presented primarily through narratives, verbatim quotes, descriptions, lists and case studies.

Qualitative methods are necessary to complement quantitative surveys, for example to understand the complexities and nuances of experiences from the respondent's point of view. Qualitative methods can be used for in-depth studies, as well as rapid assessments, and are particularly appropriate for exploratory research or when an issue is being studied for the first time. In addition, qualitative research findings are useful in assessing women's needs and constraints, community needs, designing prevention campaigns, planning and evaluating interventions and engaging community actors via participatory research.

When qualitative research is carried out in order to strengthen local programmes, the process of conducting research can initiate a public discussion about violence against women and open a dialogue with key institutional actors. For example, the Pan American Health Organization carried out a study in 10 Latin American countries that used qualitative methods to understand what happened to women affected by family violence when they decided to seek assistance.[220] The study asked: to whom does the woman turn for help? What kinds of attitudes and responses does she encounter from institutional actors? What factors motivate her to act or inhibit her from acting? The results of the study and the dissemination process served as an effective point of entry for developing coordinated community interventions against domestic violence in 25 pilot communities throughout Latin America.[221]

In another example, participatory research methods, such as focus group discussions, were used in the Dadaab refugee camp in Kenya to investigate a reported increase in cases of sexual violence and to identify possible interventions. The study found that the majority of rapes occurred when women left the camp to search for firewood. As a result, practical measures were taken to give women greater protection when they were collecting firewood.[222]

Evaluation research

Although the number and breadth of interventions to address violence against women have greatly increased in the last decade, there has been a lack of rigorous evaluation to identify the most effective practices. Very few studies have evaluated the impact on women's safety and well-being of such measures as protection orders, mandatory arrests and treatment programmes for perpetrators. Randomized control trials are considered to be the most rigorous way to compare the effectiveness of one intervention over another. However, this method is rarely used to evaluate interventions to prevent violence against women and ensure women's safety, partly due to ethical considerations. In the absence of reliable data, scarce resources might be wasted on pro-grammes that have limited impact, making investment in programme evaluation an urgent priority.[223]

Forms of violence against women that are under-documented

Although the knowledge base about all forms of violence against women needs to be strengthened, some progress has been made in documenting some of the most common forms, particularly intimate partner violence, sexual violence, female genital mutilation/cutting and child sexual abuse. However, there are still many forms of violence that remain largely undocumented. Some forms may affect relatively few women overall, but have a devastating effect on the women concerned. Some forms may be new or newly recognized. Efforts are ongoing to improve the quality of data collection, but in some cases, new methods need to be developed in order to adequately understand the extent and dynamics of these under-documented forms of violence.

Under-documented forms of violence against women include femicide; sexual violence against women in armed conflict and post-conflict situations; trafficking in women for sexual and other exploita-tion; harmful traditional practices (other than female genital mutila-tion/cutting); prenatal sex selection and neglect of infant girls; forced marriage; early marriage; acid throwing, dowry or "honour" related violence; stalking; sexual harassment and violence in custody, work-places and educational settings; and economic violence. It also includes violence against certain groups of women, for example, members of ethnic minorities, women with disabilities and migrant and undocu-mented women. Some of these were not widely recognized as forms of violence against women before the Fourth World Conference on Women in Beijing in 1995. Many of these forms of violence could be addressed in population-based surveys—for example, the WHO multi-country study on domestic violence asks detailed information about issues such as age and circumstances of marriage, the type of ceremony held and whether money was exchanged. Data collection implications for some forms are discussed below.

Femicide

Recent studies on femicide have found that the characteristics of mur-ders of women are very different from those of men and often involve domestic violence, extreme jealousy and possessiveness or passion, dowry disputes or issues of "honour". Further, they are often accompa-nied by sexual violence, as seen in recent high rates of murders of women reported in parts of Mexico and Guatemala.[224]

Studies of femicide have relied primarily on records provided by the police, the courts or medical examiners. Such records have been used to determine the relationship between the victim and the perpetra-tor (for example, intimate partners, family members or in-laws or strangers) and the circumstances of death (for example, cause of death and location).[225] Some countries categorize so-called "honour" killings or dowry murders separately, which allows researchers to examine risk factors and dynamics of these killings. However, these crimes are gen-erally considered to be grossly underreported.[226]

In most countries, police and forensic data regarding homi-cides are incomplete, and often do not provide basic information about circumstances of death or the relation between victim and perpetrator. In many countries, homicide data are not even disaggregated by the sex of the victim. Researchers have used innovative methods such as "ver-bal autopsies", which involve interviews with individuals close to the victim, to determine the circumstances of deaths and to learn how they might have been prevented.[227] In South Africa, researchers addressed the under-recording of femicide in police records by reviewing records from a variety of sources, including private mortuaries.[228]

Sexual violence against women in armed conflict and post-conflict situations

Although rape in war has been widespread for centuries, it has only recently been recognized as a significant human rights issue. Providing reliable data on the extent of sexual violence in war and humanitarian crises is particularly challenging precisely because of the chaotic circumstances and constantly shifting populations as well as safety considerations. Moreover, many women are reluctant to disclose rape, even in order to access support or obtain justice, either for fear of additional reprisals or because of the stigma associated with sexual violence.

Most of the data available on sexual violence in conflict comes from case studies or interviews with victims/survivors. Population-based surveys have been performed in a few countries, either in refugee camps or other post-conflict settings, including in Liberia, Rwanda, Sierra Leone and Timor-Leste.[229] Surveillance of sexual violence in conflict and post-conflict situations, with due attention to ethical and safety considerations, is needed urgently in order to establish more effective prevention measures and remedial services.

From 2000 to 2004, the Reproductive Health Response in Conflict Consortium spearheaded a global initiative on gender-based violence. One of its outcomes was a qualitative assessment of such violence in conflict settings. The Consortium also developed tools for measuring the prevalence of sexual violence among refugees, internally displaced persons and other conflict-affected populations.[230] The Gender-based Violence Tools Manual for Assessment and Program Design, Monitoring and Evaluation contains a series of qualitative assessment tools and techniques and a working draft of a standardized population-based survey designed to measure multiple forms of gender-based violence in conflict-affected settings around the world. This has been piloted in four countries to date.

Ending violence against women: From words to action

Trafficking in women and girls[231]

Statistics available in this area are notoriously unreliable. Many countries do not have trafficking legislation or have legislation that is inadequate. Even where legislation is in place, few traffickers are successfully prosecuted. There is often no centralized agency collecting data on human trafficking. Statistics may be reported by individual government agencies, by NGOs, the media or international or regional organizations, but these data sources are rarely linked and are often not comparable.

Trafficked women rarely report their situation to the authorities and are often unwilling to cooperate with law enforcement officials if identified and rescued. Their reasons include: fear of reprisals from traffickers; lack of trust in the authorities; the belief that the authorities cannot, or will not help; rejection by their families; and lack of opportunities in their home countries. Some trafficked women may not see themselves as exploited, particularly if they are earning more than they could in their own country.

IOM, in a review of trafficking in women across Europe, came to the conclusion that it was "not possible with any level of accuracy to produce accurate estimates for trafficking in women".[232] Most estimates on trafficking are difficult to compare or verify because the methodology for computing the estimates is rarely given, and the coverage of estimates is often unclear.[233] There is often a wide disparity between estimates, with some 10 times higher than others.

With regard to trafficking, several regional and national initiatives have begun to develop comprehensive databases to provide information on international trafficking routes, sources, transit and destination countries and on the numbers of trafficked victims and offenders.[234]

Sexual harassment and violence in workplaces and schools

The main source of information on sexual harassment in the workplace in most countries is the ministry of labour or the national office that processes complaints against employers. In countries where there is no legislation to address sexual harassment, there are virtually no records on its extent. Regardless of data collection procedures, the actual number of women who experience sexual harassment is likely to exceed by far the number of reported cases.

In many industrialized countries, surveys have been conducted to estimate the proportion of individuals who have experienced harassment, either in the workplace or educational settings. In developing countries, although harassment is recognized as a grave problem, most information comes from anecdotal, or qualitative, research and little is known about the magnitude of the problem. Only a few studies, mostly conducted in Africa, have measured the prevalence of school-based violence against girls in representative samples of students.[235]

Violence in institutional settings and correctional facilities

While there is anecdotal information, there is little data available about violence against women in health facilities,[236] including mental health facilities. Similarly, information about violence against women in prisons, detention centres and other correctional facilities is not readily available. Such information would need to be collected primarily by ministries of health and justice, as well as independent research institutions.

Indicators on violence against women

Policymakers and activists have called on States, intergovernmental bodies and others to develop a set of international indicators on violence against women. These are needed for three main purposes:

a. To persuade policymakers of the need to take action to address violence against women: the most compelling evidence has been based on household surveys that measure the extent and characteristics of different forms of violence against women. There are numerous examples around the world in which the presentation of survey data on violence against women has galvanized political will and resulted in legislative and policy reforms;

b. To measure access and quality of services to survivors of violence: this information is generally derived from the administrative records of the criminal justice system, health and social services or of NGOs that provide services to survivors of violence or from research on women's perceptions and use of services. Evaluation research, using both qualitative and quantitative methods, is key to assessing the effectiveness of programmes;

c. To monitor the progress of States in meeting their international obligations to address violence against women: relevant indicators would measure the impact of policies through changes in the prevalence and incidence of violence, progress in the establishment of legal and policy reforms, availability of services and budgetary allocations to address violence against women.

There is still no consensus as to the best approach for measuring the global occurrence of violence against women, despite several proposals for a set of international indicators.[237] The Special Rapporteur on violence against women, its causes and consequences has been invited to put forward proposals for such indicators.[238] The Millennium Project Task Force on Education and Gender Equality (Task Force 3) proposed an indicator on violence against women in order to monitor global progress in the Millennium Development Goal of "achieving gender equality and empowering women".[239]

There has also been discussion of including an indicator on violence against women in a composite index on the gender equality dimensions of human development, such as the Gender Development Index or the Gender Empowerment Measure.[240] This approach would highlight the issue of violence against women as a critical dimension of women's empowerment and place it within the broader context of human development. Including violence against women as part of a composite index would also encourage Governments to collect data on the issue.

For a composite index, a single indicator must be selected that is both simple and easy to interpret and for which robust, comparable data are available. It must also be possible to measure changes in the situation within a medium to long-term time frame. To date, the most widely available indicator is the prevalence of physical intimate partner violence, defined as the proportion of women who have ever had a partner who have experienced such violence within the last 12 months or in their lifetime. There is fairly broad consensus among researchers about how to measure physical partner violence, and it is currently included in most surveys on violence against women. For the purpose of policy development, other indicators are necessary, such as the lifetime prevalence of violence, the number, frequency and severity of violent incidents and the prevalence of other forms of violence such as sexual and emotional violence. With sufficient investment of resources and effort, an internationally comparable database could be built within the next five to seven years showing 12-month prevalence estimates of physical intimate partner violence for the majority of countries.

Improving data collection on violence against women

There is an urgent need to strengthen the knowledge base on all forms of violence against women to inform policy and strategy development. The expert group meeting on challenges and gaps in data collection on violence against women made a detailed set of recommendations for improving data collection.[241] The expert group emphasized the responsibility of States to ensure the systematic collection and publication of data, including through supporting NGOs, academics and other actors engaged in research. National statistical agencies and relevant ministries such as those of health or justice, have an important role to play in setting technical and ethical standards, ensuring consistency of concepts, regularity of data collection, and wide and timely dissemination of data. Government's national machineries for the advancement of women should be closely associated with such efforts.

Because the international understanding of what constitutes violence against women continues to evolve, operational definitions need to remain flexible. Collaboration between producers and users of data should be strengthened by having users involved in the development and implementation of data collection. Data collection on violence against women should be carried out in consultation with a wide range of stakeholders, including data suppliers, advocates and agencies providing services to women, policymakers, legislators and researchers.■

VI. THE RESPONSIBILITY OF THE STATE TO ADDRESS VIOLENCE AGAINST WOMEN

Introduction

The present section builds on section II, which summarizes the emergence of violence against women as a human rights concern and the common understanding of the State's responsibility to prevent and respond to such violence. It elaborates on the content of this responsibility and implementation at the national level.

Human rights treaties, equally applicable to women and men, set out a series of rights that are critical in the protection of women from violence (*see box 5*). These include the right to life, liberty and security of the person; to be free from torture and from cruel, inhuman or degrading treatment or punishment; to be free from slavery and servitude; to equal protection under the law; to equality in marriage and family relations; to an adequate standard of living; to just and favourable conditions of work; and to the highest attainable standard of physical and mental health.[242]

The Protocol to Prevent, Suppress and Punish Trafficking in Persons, Especially Women and Children, supplementing the United Nations Convention against Transnational Organized Crime, supports action to prevent and combat trafficking, protect and assist the victims of such trafficking and promote cooperation among States parties.

International humanitarian law is of primary relevance to the protection of women and girls during armed conflict and international criminal law and the principle of universal jurisdiction can provide an avenue of redress to women for crimes committed against them in wars and other situations of conflict and persecution.[243] International refugee law instruments, particularly the 1951 Convention relating to the Status of Refugees and its 1967 Protocol, provide protection to refugee women.

The rights of women are specifically elaborated in international and regional treaties, in particular the Convention on the Elimination of All Forms of Discrimination against Women. The Optional Protocol to the Convention, in force since 2000, establishes an individual complaints procedure as well as an inquiry procedure. Both procedures have already been used to enhance State accountability for violence against women.

While the Convention does not explicitly address violence against women (*see sect. II*), the Committee on the Elimination of Discrimination against Women made it clear that gender-based violence may breach specific provisions of the Convention regardless of whether those provisions expressly mention violence. The Convention requires "States parties to act to protect women against violence of any kind occurring within the family, at the work place or in any other area of social life".[244] The protection of women's right to be free from violence under the Convention is confirmed by the practice of States parties who report on violence against women to the Committee and the inclusion of this issue in the concluding comments of the Committee.

The Convention of Belém do Pará is the only treaty directed solely at eliminating violence against women and has frequently been cited as a model for a binding treaty on violence against women. The Protocol to the African Charter on Human and Peoples' Rights on the Rights of Women in Africa addresses violence against women within many of its provisions. In South Asia, States have agreed to the South Asian Association for Regional Cooperation Convention on Preventing and Combating the Trafficking in Women and Children for Prostitution and the Dhaka Declaration for Eliminating Violence against Women in South Asia. The provisions of the European Convention for the Protection of Human Rights and Fundamental Freedoms have also been applied in cases involving violence against women.

The international legal framework is complemented by an extensive array of policy instruments that provide detailed guidance for action to address violence against women. These include declarations and resolutions adopted by United Nations bodies and documents emanating from United Nations conferences and summit meetings (*see box 5*).

Human rights treaty bodies established to monitor the implementation of treaties—the Committee on the Elimination of Discrimination against Women, the Human Rights Committee, the Committee on Economic, Social and Cultural Rights, the Committee on the Elimination of Racial Discrimination, the Committee on the Rights of the Child, the Committee Against Torture and the Committee on Migrant Workers—address violence against women in relation to the enjoyment of the rights protected by the respective treaties. The treaty bodies address the structural causes of violence against women and clarify States' obligations to address and prevent all forms of violence against women in general recommendations and concluding observations and in their work under individual complaints and inquiry procedures. Other United Nations mechanisms, in particular the Special Rapporteur on violence against women, its causes and consequences, contribute to the understanding of State responsibility for preventing and eliminating violence against women.

There is an increasing body of jurisprudence on violence against women at the international and regional level. In particular, case law has been established by the European and inter-American human rights systems and by the ad hoc international criminal tribunals (*see box 10*). These decisions set important precedents on the applicability of international law to State and individual responsibility for violence against women.

Legislative and judicial developments at the national level have also elaborated on standards of State responsibility within national contexts. The Constitutional Court of South Africa, for example, has held that the State has a duty under international law to protect women from gender-based discrimination, including violence that has the purpose or effect of impairing the enjoyment by women of their human rights.[245]

The implementation of international norms and standards on violence against women requires comprehensive legal, policy and other measures at the national level, with the involvement of many stakeholders. These include all levels of the State at federal, state, provincial and local levels, as well as all branches of Government, including the judiciary, legislature and executive. Collaboration and coordination between all stakeholders, including Governments, NGOs and civil society organizations are vital for an effective approach to redressing such violence (*see sect. VII*).

Box 10
Examples of international and regional jurisprudence on violence against women

International

- *Kisoki v. Sweden*, Communication No. 41/1996 (A/51/44), Committee against Torture

- *The Prosecutor v. Jean-Paul Akayesu*, Case No. ICTR-96-4-T-2, 1998, International Criminal Tribunal for Rwanda

- *The Prosecutor v. Dragoljub Kunarac, Radomir Kovac, and Zoran Vukovic*, Case No. IT-96-23&23/1, 2002, International Criminal Tribunal for the former Yugoslavia

- *Karen Noelia Llantoy Huamán v. Peru*, Communication No. 1153/2003, Human Rights Committee

- *AT v. Hungary*, Communication No. 2/2003, 2005, Committee on the Elimination of Discrimination against Women

- *Inquiry under article 8 of the Optional Protocol to the Convention on the Elimination of All Forms of Discrimination against Women in regard to Mexico, and reply from the Government of Mexico*, 2005, Committee on the Elimination of Discrimination against Women (See CEDAW/C/2005/OP.8/Mexico.)

Regional

- *Airey v. Ireland*, European Court of Human Rights, 6289/73, 1979

- *X and Y v. the Netherlands*, European Court of Human Rights, 8978/80, 1985

- *Raquel Martí de Mejía v. Peru*, Inter-American Commission on Human Rights, Case 10.970, 1996

- *Aydin v. Turkey*, European Court of Human Rights, 23178/94, 1997

- *Ana, Beatriz and Celia Gonzáles Pérez v. Mexico*, Inter-American Commission on Human Rights, Case 11.565, No. 53/01, 2000

- *María da Penha Maia Fernandes v. Brazil*, Inter-American Commission on Human Rights, Case 12.051, 2001

- *Algür v. Turkey*, European Court of Human Rights, 32574/96, 2002

- *María Mamérita Mestanza Chávez v. Peru*, Inter-American Commission on Human Rights, Case 12.191, 2003

- *MC v. Bulgaria*, European Court of Human Rights, 39272/98, 2003

State responsibility

It is now well established under international law that violence against women is a form of discrimination against women and a violation of human rights.[246] States' obligations to respect, protect, fulfil and promote human rights[247] with regard to violence against women encompasses the responsibility to prevent, investigate and prosecute all forms of, and protect women from, such violence and to hold perpetrators accountable.[248]

States are responsible under international law for human rights violations and acts of violence against women perpetrated by the State or any of its agents.[249] Such responsibility arises not only from State actions, but also from omissions and failure to take positive measures to protect and promote rights.[250] States must refrain from committing human rights violations through their own agents. They also have a duty to prevent human rights violations by non-State actors, investigate allegations of violations, punish wrongdoers and provide effective remedies to victims. States are accountable for the actions of non-State actors if they fail to act with due diligence to prevent, investigate or punish such acts and provide an effective remedy.[251]

Much violence against women is committed by private actors and includes a broad range of individuals and entities, such as intimate partners and other family members; casual acquaintances and strangers; neighbourhood and community institutions; criminal gangs, organizations and business enterprises. The use of the standard of due diligence underlines the State's duty to protect women effectively from such violence.

The standard of due diligence is articulated in general recommendation No. 19 of the Committee on the Elimination of Discrimination against Women, which notes that "States may also be responsible for private acts if they fail to act with due diligence to prevent violations of rights or to investigate and punish acts of violence, and for providing compensation" and in international and regional legal and policy instruments[252] and jurisprudence. In *Velasquez Rodriguez v. Honduras*,[253] the Inter-American Court of Human Rights held that a State must take action to prevent human rights violations committed by non-State actors, investigate allegations of violations and punish wrongdoers. The standard is not one of strict liability, in which the State would be held accountable for acts of violence against women regardless of the circumstances, but rather one of reasonableness.[254] It is based on principles of non-discrimination and good faith in application.[255] The standard of due diligence therefore requires a State to act with the existing means at its disposal to address both individual acts of violence against women and the structural causes so as to prevent future violence.[256]

When State actors commit sexual violence, such violence may constitute torture. For example, the rape of women in custody by State agents including soldiers, policemen and prison officers has been recognized as an act of torture. The Committee against Torture found that a woman would be in danger of being tortured if returned to Zaire, where she was allegedly raped by security forces.[257] The European Court of Human Rights held that physical and mental abuse of a woman in detention violated her right to freedom from torture or inhuman or degrading treatment or punishment.[258] The Inter-American Commission on Human Rights found that a family of four women who were beaten and gang-raped by Mexican military personnel in detention had been tortured.[259]

The International Criminal Tribunals for the former Yugoslavia and Rwanda have recognized sexual violence including rape as acts of torture, as crimes against humanity and an element of genocide in some circumstances.[260] The Rwanda tribunal recognized that "sexual violence is not limited to physical invasion of the human body and may include acts which do not involve penetration or even physical contact".[261] The Special Court for Sierra Leone included forced marriage in an indictment.[262] The Rome Statute of the International Criminal Court established jurisdiction to try crimes of sexual violence, such as rape, sexual slavery, enforced prostitution and forced pregnancy, enforced sterilization and other sexual violence as crimes against humanity when committed as part of a widespread or systematic attack directed at a civilian population.[263]

The international legal and policy frameworks provide a set of standards for action by States to prevent and eliminate violence against women. Different contexts, circumstances and constraints, including availability of resources, will affect the type of action to be taken. Inaction or inadequate action results in a breach of a State's duty to address such violence. Examples are provided below.

Addressing violence against women

Measures taken to prevent violence against women, to investigate and prosecute acts of violence and punish perpetrators and to put in place remedies are benchmarks by which States, women's organizations and advocates and human rights mechanisms may assess national laws, programmes and policies and evaluate their compliance with international obligations. States have a general duty to promote de facto equality between women and men and to develop and implement effectively a legal and policy framework for the full protection and promotion of women's human rights. This is particularly important where women may face increased risk of violence because their enjoyment of rights such as those to housing, education or employment is impaired. State responsibility is not limited to responding to acts of violence against women, but extends to identifying patterns of inequality that could result in violence and taking steps to overcome them.

Legal and policy framework

Adherence to the Convention on the Elimination of All Forms of Discrimination against Women, its Optional Protocol and other relevant international human rights treaties and the removal of reservations constitute measures to address violence against women.[264] Similarly, the inclusion of the principle of equality of men and women in national constitutions or similar legislation, in accordance with international standards, enhances the framework for addressing violence against women.[265] National plans of action to protect women against violence and to improve the promotion and protection of women's human rights are part of compliance measures.[266] States are also required to allocate an adequate budget to address violence against women.[267]

The requirement to enact, implement and monitor legislation covering all forms of violence against women is set out in a number of international and regional instruments.[268] It has been elaborated in the case of *AT v. Hungary*,[269] where the Committee on the Elimination of Discrimination against Women found that the lack of specific legislation to combat domestic violence and sexual harassment constituted a violation of human rights and fundamental freedoms, particularly the right to security of person. In *X and Y v. the Netherlands*,[270] the European Court of Human Rights found that the Netherlands had breached its human rights responsibilities by failing to create appropriate criminal legislation applicable to the rape of a mentally handicapped young woman.

The requirement to review and revise existing laws and policy to address violence against women was spelled out by the Inter-American Commission on Human Rights in the case of *María Mamérita Mestanza Chávez v. Peru*,[271] which involved a government sterilization programme.

The case of *MC v. Bulgaria* illustrates the importance of monitoring the manner in which legislation is enforced. In this case, the European Court of Human Rights found that although the article prohibiting rape in Bulgaria's penal code did not "mention any requirement of physical resistance by the victim", physical resistance appeared to be required in practice to pursue a charge of rape.[272]

Criminal justice system

Investigation

States have a duty as set out in numerous international instruments to investigate acts of violence against women.[273] Such investigations should use techniques that do "not degrade women subjected to violence and minimize intrusion, while maintaining standards for the collection of the best evidence".[274] In *AT v. Hungary*, the Committee on the Elimination of Discrimination against Women spelled out the need to "investigate promptly, thoroughly, impartially and seriously all allegations" of domestic violence.[275] In *MC v. Bulgaria*,[276] the European Court of Human Rights upheld the positive duty of States to ensure the effectiveness of the criminal law through effective investigation and prosecution. The Court found that the approach of the prosecutors and investigators "fell short of the requirement inherent in States' positive obligations—viewed in the light of the relevant modern standards in comparative and international law—to establish and apply effectively a criminal law system punishing all forms of rape and sexual abuse".[277] The creation of a safe and confidential system for

Where adequate legislation exists, the treaty bodies have frequently expressed concern that such legislation has not been effectively implemented. Particular concerns include: the absence of regulations to implement legislation; lack of clear procedures for law enforcement and health-care personnel; attitudes of law enforcement officers that discourage women from reporting cases; high dismissal rates of cases by police and prosecutors; high withdrawal rates of complaints by victims; low prosecution rates; low conviction rates; failure of courts to apply uniform criteria, particularly in relation to measures to protect victims; lack of legal aid and high costs of legal representation in courts; practices that deny women agency, such as detaining women for their "protection" without their consent; and use of reconciliation proceedings between a perpetrator and a victim of violence in criminal and divorce cases to the detriment of the victim.

In countries where customary law prevails alongside codified law, the Committee and other treaty bodies have been consistently concerned about the use of discriminatory customary law and practice, despite laws enacted to protect women from violence.

Training

The treaty bodies have emphasized that in order for legislation and policies pertaining to violence against women to be effectively enforced, the officials responsible for implementation must be provided with training to ensure that they are sensitized to all forms of violence against women and can respond in a gender-sensitive manner.

Provision of services

The treaty bodies have expressed concern where States parties do not have sufficient support measures in place for women victims/survivors of violence. The treaty bodies have emphasized the responsibility of the State to ensure that victims/survivors have access to services such as shelters and legal, medical and psychological support. The Committee on the Elimination of Discrimination against Women has also been concerned about inadequate financing for such programmes and organizations that provide such services. It has also expressed concern about the lack of monitoring of programmes providing services to victims/ survivors of violence.

Attitudes and stereotypes

The treaty bodies have highlighted the fact that women are kept in subordinate positions and thus placed at risk of violence, by traditions and customs that discriminate against women, by gender-role stereotyping and by discrimination against women in law, including customary law and in practice. The treaty bodies have noted that the perpetuation of discriminatory attitudes and stereotypes constructs violence against women, particularly domestic violence, as a private matter that is acceptable or normal. In doing so, the treaty bodies have stressed the importance of States parties taking steps to eliminate such attitudes and stereotypes.

Data and research

The treaty bodies have been consistently concerned by the lack of systematic data collection on all forms of violence against women and the lack of data disaggregated by sex more generally.

Actions to be taken by States to meet their international obligations

The international legal and policy framework establishes standards for action by States to meet their legal obligations and policy commitments to address violence against women. These fall into the following categories:

- Ratification of all international human rights instruments, including the Convention on the Elimination of all Forms of Discrimination against Women and its Optional Protocol, and withdrawal of reservations

- Establishment of constitutional frameworks guaranteeing substantive equality for women and prohibiting violence against women

- Adoption, periodic review and effective implementation, in a gender-sensitive manner, of legislation that criminalizes all forms of violence against women

- Formulation and implementation of executive policies or plans of action to eliminate violence against women and regular monitoring and evaluation of such policies or plans of action

- Investigation in a prompt, thorough, gender-sensitive and effective manner of all allegations of violence against women, including by keeping official records of all complaints; undertaking investigation and evidence-gathering expeditiously; collecting and safeguarding evidence, with witness protection where needed; and providing the opportunity for women to make complaints to, and deal with, skilled and professional female staff

- Prosecution of the perpetrators of all forms of violence against women and elimination of any climate of impunity surrounding such offences

- Action to ensure that the criminal justice system, including rules of evidence and procedure, functions in a non-discriminating and gender-sensitive manner to encourage women's testimony in proceedings regarding violence against women

- Punishment of the perpetrators of all forms of violence against women in a manner commensurate with the severity of the offence

- Provision of appropriate remedies, including by adopting measures to allow victims to obtain appropriate symbolic and actual compensation, without prejudice to possible civil proceedings against the perpetrator

- Implementation of training and awareness-raising programmes to familiarize judges, prosecutors and other members of the legal profession with women's human rights in general, and the Convention on the Elimination of All Forms of Discrimination against Women and its Optional Protocol in particular

- Implementation of training programmes for judicial, legal, medical, social services, social work, educational, police and immigration personnel to educate such personnel and sensitize them to the social context of violence against women

- Action to eliminate all forms of discrimination against women and raise awareness of the issue of violence against women through measures such as: removing all stereotypes and sexist content from educational curricula and creating positive images of women; organizing, supporting or funding, as appropriate, community-based education campaigns to raise awareness about violence against women; promoting and instituting an active and visible policy of gender main-streaming in all policies and programmes

- Creation of services, in cooperation with civil society organizations as appropriate, in the following areas: access to justice, including free legal aid when necessary; provision of a safe and confidential environment for women to report violence against women; adequately funded shelters and relief services; adequately funded health-care and support services, including counselling; linguistically and culturally accessible services for women requiring such services; and counselling and rehabilitation programmes for perpetrators of violence against women

- Systematic collection of data disaggregated by sex and other factors such as age, ethnicity and disability detailing the prevalence of all forms of violence against women; the causes and consequences of violence against women; and the effectiveness of any measures implemented to prevent and redress violence against women.■

VII. PROMISING PRACTICES AND CHALLENGES FOR IMPLEMENTATION

Introduction

Good or promising practices have been developed by many States to meet their human rights obligations to address violence against women. Innovative work has been done by women's NGOs in many countries, sometimes in collaboration with the State, to find dynamic approaches to ending violence against women in differing contexts. It remains, however, difficult to identify best practices on an international or global level because of the range of ways and the variety of contexts in which violence against women is manifested. The lack of sustained resources committed to this work, and especially to evaluating different initiatives, adds to the difficulty of generalizing about which approach works best. For this reason, this study uses the more qualified characterization of "promising" or "good" practice.

There is as yet no agreement on assessment criteria of "good practices". Whether a practice is "good", "promising" or "effective" depends both on the standards that are used in evaluation and on the local context. Family forms, living arrangements and livelihoods and the capacities of the State vary across and within societies, leading to different approaches to tackling similar problems. What works well is influenced by the form of the State, its commitment to women's equality, its relationship with NGOs and civil society and the resources it has to draw on. Whether the State is involved in or emerging from conflict, or hosts large refugee populations is another critical factor. The challenge is to identify useful generalizations about interventions and reforms without understating the importance of the specific context and without minimizing the responsibility of the State to address violence against women despite constraints.

There are generic aspects of good or promising practices that can be extracted from a variety of experiences around the world. Common principles of such practices include: clear policies and laws that make violence illegal; strong enforcement mechanisms; effective and well-trained personnel; the involvement of multiple sectors; and close collaboration with local women's groups, civil society organizations, academics and professionals. It is critical to involve women fully and to use their experiences of violence—including the complexities that arise from multiple discrimination—as the starting point for developing policies and programmes. The most promising practices in all areas involve a clear demonstration of political commitment to eliminating violence against women, as evidenced by statements by high-level government officials, backed by action and the commitment of resources by the State.

Practices emerge in particular contexts and circumstances, often building on and learning from what has been tried before. A practice may be considered good based on its effectiveness, replicability, sustainability, relevance, responsiveness, efficiency or innovativeness.[302] The process involved in developing or implementing a practice may itself be considered a good practice. The former Special Rapporteur on violence against women described "best" or "good" practices as those "that led to actual change, contributed to a policy environment more conducive to gender equality and/or have broken new ground in non-traditional areas for women".[303]

Collaboration and coordination between Governments, NGOs and civil society organizations continue to be vital in the development of effective practices to eliminate violence against women. Examples include alliances and coalitions between Government and NGOs that draw on the experience and expertise of the most active and informed partners—women's groups and networks—in designing and implementing programmes. Coordination and networking between government sectors, such as the justice system and the health, education and employment sectors, is widely seen as good practice. The formation of strategic coalitions and alliances between groups working on violence against women and those working on other issues such as HIV/AIDS, women's economic empowerment and other aspects of social justice is also good practice.

Governments, NGOs and women's rights activists dealing with violence against women have used different approaches in three distinct, yet interrelated, areas: law and justice, provision of services and prevention of violence. Many Governments use national plans of action, which include legal measures, service provision and prevention strategies, to address violence against women. Promising practices in the development and implementation of such plans of action include consultation with women's groups and other civil society organizations, clear timelines and benchmarks, transparent mechanisms for monitoring implementation, clear indicators of impact and evaluation, predictable and adequate funding streams and the integration of measures to address and prevent violence against women in sectoral programmes.

States' responsibilities in addressing violence against women, as well as gaps in implementation, were laid out in section VI. This section indicates how these gaps in implementation at the national level could be closed by presenting examples of practices that, for different reasons, are viewed as good or promising. They are drawn mainly from experience with domestic violence and sexual violence because there is more information available in these areas, but many of the principles apply more broadly. The list of examples is neither exhaustive nor static. As experience grows, existing practices may be eclipsed by innovations and new insights that offer even more promise in efforts to prevent and redress violence against women.[304] Enhanced use of such promising practices could also respond to the consistent concerns voiced by treaty bodies (*see sect. VI*) about gaps in legislation and its effective implementation, in provision of services and in general prevention efforts.

Promising practices in law

The incorporation of provisions on gender equality in national constitutions or other comparable legislation and the elimination of discriminatory provisions in all areas of law, enhance the prevention of violence against women and constitute good practice. Laws establish standards of right and wrong, deter wrongdoers through arrests, prosecution and punishment of perpetrators and provide remedies to victims. Laws provide access to justice and may mandate the allocation of resources or the establishment of services for victims/survivors. Laws alone, however, are insufficient and need to be part of a broader effort that encompasses public policies, public education, services and violence prevention.[305]

Guiding principles for promising practices in law and the justice system

A growing body of experience suggests that when certain principles are followed, laws have greater potential to address violence against women effectively. These principles include:

- Address violence against women as a form of gender-based discrimination, linked to other forms of oppression of women, and a violation of women's human rights

- Make clear that violence against women is unacceptable and that eliminating it is a public responsibility

- Monitor implementation of legal reforms to assess how well they are working in practice

- Keep legislation under constant review and continue to reform it in the light of new information and understanding

- Ensure that victims/survivors of violence are not "revictimized" through the legal process

- Promote women's agency and empower individual women who are victims/survivors of violence

- Promote women's safety in public spaces

- Take into account the differential impact of measures on women according to their race, class, ethnicity, religion, disability, culture, indigenous or migrant status, legal status, age or sexual orientation

Legal framework

Enactment of laws

Enacting laws prohibiting specific forms of violence against women is an important step towards eliminating such violence.[306] Good practice in the development of such laws requires a process that is consultative and that incorporates the opinions of civil society, especially victims/survivors and women's NGOs, in dialogue with practitioners who will apply and enforce the laws. For example, the 2004 Spanish Protection from Violence Act (Ley Integral) was developed with strong involvement from women's organizations and contains a wide definition of violence including psychological forms of violence, such as sexual aggression, threat, compulsion, coercion and deprivation of free will.[307] The law covers preventive and educational measures, as well as protection and assistance for victims and new sanctions against perpetrators. The Mongolian Domestic Violence Law, enacted in May 2004, was the result of collaboration between two prominent Mongolian women's NGOs and the parliamentary domestic violence legislative taskforce.[308]

Implementation of laws

The potential of laws on violence against women remains unfulfilled if they are not effectively applied and enforced. Implementation of laws is enhanced by mandatory and systematic gender-sensitivity training of law enforcement officials, prosecutors and judges and by protocols and guidelines on the appropriate application of the law. Critical for the effective use of the law is women's knowledge of the law and the protection and remedies it offers and women's capacity to claim these rights effectively.

Gender-sensitivity training of law enforcement officials is conducted in many countries by Governments and civil society organizations, often in collaboration. Good practice requires such training to be systematic and mandatory. For example, Brazil and Paraguay have introduced compulsory educational curricula on violence against women for police trainees.[309] Luxembourg's Ministry for the Advancement of Women conducts training on domestic violence for members of the national police directorate, officers of the National Police Academy and the public prosecutor's office.[310] The National Police Agency in the Republic of Korea educates police officials on the laws on domestic violence, procedures in responding to reports and steps to protect victims. It also conducts a nationwide test of police officials on these subjects.[311] Chile has trained more than 25,000 officials under a framework developed by the Inter-Ministerial Commission on Violence within the Family Sphere.[312] In the Netherlands, a nationwide project on domestic violence launched by the Board of Police Commissioners in 2003 encourages all police regions to develop a policy on tackling domestic violence, to promote police expertise and to enable the national registration of domestic violence cases.[313] The Centre for Women's and Children's Studies in Bangladesh developed a training manual for police officers that reflects the needs of survivors and defines the role of law enforcement in combating domestic, sexual and dowry-related violence, trafficking and acid throwing.[314]

Programmes to enhance the gender-sensitivity of judges include "Towards a Jurisprudence of Equality", developed by the International Association of Women Judges and its partners in Africa and Latin America. This programme strengthens the capacity of judges and magistrates to apply international and regional human rights law to cases involving violence against women.[315] The Indian women's NGO Sakshi has trained members of the judiciary on gender issues using interactive dialogue, small group problem-solving, visits to shelters and meetings with NGOs to give judges a better understanding of women's experiences.[316] Women in Law and Development Africa, an NGO, has compiled legal training kits for judges.[317] The Gender Justice Awards organized by the Government of the Philippines in collaboration with civil society recognize judges who have rendered gender-sensitive decisions in cases of violence against women.[318]

Guidelines and protocols on the implementation of laws and policies regarding violence against women have been devised in several countries. Such guidelines and protocols are promising practice in that they establish clear and predictable standards to follow for the police and others who respond to violence against women. The South African Police Service and the National Prosecuting Authority have compiled detailed documents setting out standards for the management of domestic violence and sexual assault cases.[319] In the United Kingdom, there are guidelines for police, social workers and educational professionals on addressing forced marriages.[320]

Programmes and strategies to empower women by raising their awareness about their rights and enhancing their capacity to claim such rights have been developed in many countries, mostly by NGOs. Such programmes can also contribute to increased reporting of violence. In 2004, the Afghan Women's Resource Center trained more than 500 women in a remote area of Afghanistan about their basic rights, violence against women and forced marriages. In Timor-Leste, Fokupers, an NGO, provides accessible legal aid services for women victims and raises public awareness of domestic violence and women's legal rights. Its Babadok Bulletin and public information brochures are distributed to service providers, religious institutions, government agencies and lawmakers.

Monitoring laws

Good practice involves monitoring and evaluating laws to ensure continuing effective application through such mechanisms as ombudspersons, national rapporteurs, observatories and gender equality machinery. For example, Nepal and the Netherlands have national rapporteurs on trafficking who oversee and monitor anti-trafficking activities.[321]

Civil society organizations play a fundamental role in monitoring the implementation of legislation and policy. The European Women's Lobby, the largest umbrella organization of women's associations in the European Union, established the European Observatory on Violence against Women in 1997.[322] The Observatory is composed of women experts from each of the European Union member States who monitor policy issues at the national, European, and international levels and share good practices identified. In addition, five European countries have now established national observatories.[323]

Periodic review and revision of laws

Good practice requires periodic review and reform of laws taking account of the evolving knowledge-base on violence against women and the ways to address it, developments in international human rights law and insights gained through application, monitoring and evaluation. The Convention of Belém do Pará led to the enactment of laws on violence against women in countries in the Latin American region. Insights gained from the application of such laws have resulted in their revision, including revision of domestic violence laws, such as in Belize, Peru and Puerto Rico, to enhance their applicability and effectiveness.[324]

Evolving knowledge has led to the inclusion of new standards in legislation. In Canada, a person charged with sexual violence is now required to have taken reasonable steps to determine whether there was consent, as opposed to the victim having to establish resistance.[325] The marital rape exemption has been removed from the laws in many countries and marital rape has been criminalized in others (*see box 1*).

Reduced penalties in cases of "honour killings" have been eliminated in Tunisia,[326] and crimes committed in the name of "honour" are punishable by life imprisonment in Turkey.[327] Psychological and economic violence are now incorporated in the legal definition of domestic violence in a number of countries including Costa Rica, Guatemala, Honduras and South Africa.[328.]

Criminal law

Prosecution and punishment of perpetrators

Vigorous arrest and prosecution policies make a statement to society as a whole that violence against women is a serious crime that is not condoned by the authorities. However, the majority of reported cases of violence against women are not prosecuted and of those that are, many do not result in a conviction. Even when perpetrators are convicted, they often receive sentences that are not commensurate with the gravity of the crime.[329]

Measures that enhance women's access to justice, including timely arrests, effective proceedings and punishments are good practice. An inter-agency project, the Family Violence Intervention Program, in Canberra, Australia, works with prosecutors to ensure that they do not drop domestic violence cases. It uses an agreed protocol between involved agencies and technology such as digital cameras to photograph victims and crime scenes, making evidence available to the court. Since the inception of the project, there has been a 288 per cent increase in cases prosecuted.[330]

Appropriate sentencing can be achieved through the introduction of minimum sentences for certain offences and monitoring of sentencing practices. Several States, such as Sri Lanka, have minimum prison sentences for rape and aggravated rape.[331] The Solicitor General in the United Kingdom monitors all sentencing and may refer cases to the Court of Criminal Appeal when the sentence is considered too lenient.

Protection of victims' rights

Women victims of violence frequently do not seek justice because of feelings of shame and fear of persecution by the criminal justice system.[332] Good practice involves safeguarding the rights of victims and creating a system that respects the privacy, dignity and autonomy of all victims and is conducive to reporting.

A number of States have endeavoured to meet such objectives by providing greater legal protection for victims of rape, including through laws that prevent the introduction of unrelated evidence about a victim's sexual behaviour in order to protect victims of rape from abusive cross-examination. The Philippines Rape Victim Assistance and Protection Act of 1998 is one example. Courtroom procedures that protect the privacy of victims during trial, such as allowing evidence to be given by video link or restricting access to courtrooms for the general public during rape trials, are used increasingly widely, including in Finland, Ireland, Japan and Nepal.[333]

Progress has been made in a number of areas to avoid the re-victimization of women in the criminal justice process. For example, "virginity tests" in rape cases have been banned in Jordan and Turkey.[334] Provisions allowing impunity for rape if the perpetrator marries the victim have been removed from the penal codes of countries including Egypt,[335] Costa Rica, Ethiopia, Peru,[336] and Turkey.[337]

Civil remedies

Civil laws complement criminal measures and play an important role in providing victims/survivors with avenues of redress and compensation. Promising practice in this area includes the availability of civil remedies such as civil protection orders; anti-discrimination laws; civil laws to sue perpetrators and State agents for compensation; and victim compensation funds that cover cases of violence against women.

Protection orders, also known as restraining or removal orders, aim to protect women from the immediate threat of violence by restraining the perpetrator from contacting the victim during a specified period or removing the perpetrator from the home. Such orders have been adopted in countries around the world. Under the Austrian Federal Act on Protection against Family Violence, the police may immediately evict and bar the batterer from the home of the victim for 10 to 20 days. Longer-term protection is available through a court-issued protective temporary injunction.[338] This law has been replicated in other European countries, including Germany.[339]

Under the general tort law of most countries, women may bring a civil action for assault, battery or the intentional infliction of emotional distress, although this is not often done. Civil suits may result in financial compensation for the harm inflicted. Victims/survivors of violence, or families of the deceased, may pursue civil causes of action not only against the perpetrators but also against law enforcement officials when they fail to provide adequate protection to individual victims.[340]

Anti-discrimination laws and laws that identify violence against women as a violation of women's civil rights are promising in that they convey the message that acts of violence against women are not merely crimes by one individual against another but are an assault on a publicly shared ideal of equal rights.[341] Some States and localities within the United States, such as New York state, have enacted laws providing a remedy for acts of violence against women as a violation of civil rights.[342] The South African Promotion of Equality and Prevention of Unfair Discrimination Act explicitly recognizes gender-based violence as unfair discrimination and requires the State and non-State actors to refrain from discriminating and to take positive measures to promote equality. Sexual harassment is recognized as a form of discrimination and a violation of women's human rights in several States, including New Zealand.

Specialized laws and procedures to address violence against women

The adoption of specialized laws and procedures on violence against women is promising in that such laws and procedures aim to enhance the effectiveness of the State's response to violence against women. Some States have enacted comprehensive laws specific to violence against women that provide multiple types of remedy. For example, in the United States, the federal Violence against Women Act of 1994 contains provisions designed to reduce the frequency of violence against women, provide needed services to victims, hold perpetrators accountable, strengthen law enforcement, improve research and data collection and reform immigration law to help battered immigrant women escape their abusers. The statute authorized the appropriation of more than 1 billion United States dollars ($) in federal funds to support a broad range of programmes, including training police, prosecutors and judges; supporting shelters and rape prevention programmes; setting up a national toll-free domestic violence telephone hotline; and establishing a national database to improve the ability of local, state and federal law enforcement agencies to record and share information.[343] In the Philippines, the Anti-Violence against Women and Their Children Act of 2004 criminalizes acts of physical, sexual, psychological and economic abuse in intimate relationships. The law allows courts to issue temporary protection orders and, for rural women, mandates village officials to provide protection. The law also created an inter-agency council to formulate programmes and projects.[344]

Specialized courts can improve efficiency, minimize the burden on victims and improve case outcomes when prosecutors, judges and other court officers have received relevant training. These courts take many different forms and the most ambitious combine different components of the legal system, such as civil and criminal, as well as non-legal aspects such as access to support services and counselling. A model Integrated Domestic Violence Court developed in the United States in New York state has been replicated in other parts of the world, including the United Kingdom.[345] In South Africa, 54 specialist Sexual Offences Courts have been established, which have greatly reduced case turnaround time and increased conviction rates.[346]

Specialized police units aim to provide a safe environment for women who report violence and to enhance the police response to violence against women through specialized officers. The first women's police unit was established in Sao Paulo, Brazil in 1985.[347] The practice then spread throughout Latin America, including to Argentina, Ecuador, Peru and Uruguay.[348] In the Dominican Republic, domestic violence legislation is enforced by six prosecutor's offices working exclusively with domestic violence cases; six police squads specifically charged with protecting women from violence; and a magistrate's court and a criminal court dealing exclusively with cases of domestic violence.[349] In Belgium, the Human Trafficking Unit is tasked with detecting cases of human trafficking, sending early warnings to the authorities and serving as an operational focal point within the country's police forces.[350]

Other areas of law

Because violence affects every aspect of a woman's life, it is good practice to scrutinize the many other areas of law that may affect victims/survivors. Women's rights advocates have worked to incorporate a sensitivity to violence against women in such diverse areas of law as divorce, child custody and visitation, child abuse and neglect, welfare and public benefits, immigration, employment and housing. Even the best laws providing civil and criminal remedies for violence against women are of limited utility if victims are placed at a disadvantage by other legal rules.[351] For example, a migrant woman who is subjected to domestic violence but is dependent on her husband's immigration status is unlikely to report it for fear of repercussions. Countries such as Canada, the Netherlands and the United States have addressed this concern by allowing victims of domestic violence to apply for permanent residence status irrespective of whether their spouses support their application.

The application of international law by national courts

The use of international legal standards on violence against women by domestic courts is a promising practice. In a case where a woman was attacked by a man on bail on a rape charge, the South African Constitutional Court held that the police and prosecutors had failed to comply with a legal duty to take steps to prevent him from causing her harm.[352] In rejecting a challenge to the constitutionality of key provisions of domestic violence legislation, the Court held that it was the duty of the State under international law, including the Convention on the Elimination of All Forms of Discrimination against Women, to enact appropriate and effective legislation. The Supreme Court of India[353] relied on the Indian Government's international obligations, particularly under the Convention on the Elimination of All Forms of Discrimination against Women and the Beijing Platform for Action, to establish guidelines and norms on sexual harassment at work. These norms were to be observed pending the enactment of appropriate national legislation.

Box 11
National laws on violence against women

Over the past decade, many States have introduced laws addressing various forms of violence against women. States' responsibility for the enactment of a legal framework for addressing all forms of violence against women was discussed in section 6, as were the concerns of treaty bodies about persistent gaps. The present box highlights existing legislation in five areas where treaty bodies have commonly voiced concerns.[a] The information was last updated on 30 April 2006.

Domestic violence

Eighty-nine States currently have some legislative provisions that specifically address domestic violence. Of these, 60 States have specific domestic violence laws; seven have violence against women laws; one has a gender-neutral law against violence; 14 have specific provisions on domestic violence in their penal codes; five have civil procedures for the removal of perpetrators; and one addresses domestic violence through family law. Twelve of the States with specific domestic violence legislation refer to family-based violence rather than gender-based violence. There are 102 States that are not known to have any specific legal provisions on domestic violence. Twenty States have draft legislation on domestic violence in varying stages of development, with a further four states having expressed an intention to develop specific legislation, or provisions, on domestic violence.

Marital rape

Marital rape may be prosecuted in at least 104 States.[b] Of these, 32 have made marital rape a specific criminal offence, while the remaining 74 do not exempt marital rape from general rape provisions. Marital rape is not a prosecutable offence in at least 53 States. Four States criminalize marital rape only when the spouses are judicially separated. Four States are considering legislation that would allow marital rape to be prosecuted.

Sexual harassment

Ninety States[c] have some form of legislative provision against sexual harassment. Of these, 11 States have adopted specific legislation on sexual harassment; another 31 States have amended their penal code or criminal law to make sexual harassment a specific criminal offence; 18 States address sexual harassment in their labour code or employment law; 18 States address it in anti-discrimination or gender equality legislation; and 12 States have a combination of provisions in these three areas. In addition, the judiciaries of two States have developed common law doctrines on sexual harassment.[d] Seven States are considering draft laws pertaining to sexual harassment.

Trafficking

A total of 93 States have some legislative provision regarding trafficking in human beings. Of these, 10 States have legislative provisions that apply only to children. Currently, there are at least 7 States with draft legislation regarding trafficking.

Female genital mutilation/cutting

Fifteen of the 28 African States where female genital mutilation/cutting is prevalent have enacted laws criminalizing the practice. In addition, one State has enacted a health law prohibiting female genital mutilation/cutting, two prohibit the practice through ministerial decrees and in one federal State, several states criminalize the practice. Five additional African States are considering draft legislation on female genital mutilation/cutting. Of the nine States in Asia and the Arabian Peninsula where female genital mutilation/cutting is prevalent among certain groups, two have enacted legal measures prohibiting it. In addition, 10 States in other parts of the world have enacted laws criminalizing the practice.

---

[a] Research was conducted on the laws of 191 States. The main sources were State reports under the Convention; Member States' responses to the questionnaire for the ten-year review and appraisal of the Beijing Platform for Action and Outcome Document; Member States' contributions to the Secretary-General's study; reports of the Special Rapporteur on violence against women, its causes and consequences; ILO reports; reports of non-governmental organizations; and Government websites.

[b] The following figures on marital rape do not include 16 States for which information could not be found.

[c] Some legislative measures regarding sexual harassment are not all-encompassing in their scope. For example, some States have legislation directed solely towards public sector employees, while others address sexual harassment in their morality laws.

[d] *Vishaka v. State of Rajasthan and others AIR*, 1997 S.C. 3011 (India); and *Bank Employees' Union v. Republic Bank Ltd.* Trade Dispute 17 of 1995 (Trinidad and Tobago).

Promising practices in the provision of services

All over the world, women suffer the physical, emotional and psychological effects of violence. They also have to face the economic and social consequences that affect their lives, relationships, productivity and achievement in education and employment. Victims/survivors of violence against women need timely access to health care and support services that respond to short-term injuries, protect them from further violations and address longer-term needs. Yet many do not get the help they need, because there are too few support services in their country, because they do not have access to services or do not know about their existence or because, for whatever reason, they are reluctant to contact those services. Good practices in the provision of services endeavour to address these challenges.

Support services are provided by a range of actors, most commonly by State agencies and NGOs. Communities, employers, private practitioners and individuals may also provide support. Support for victims/survivors needs State funding and encouragement and benefits from State coordination with NGO initiatives. It requires training and capacity-building across State agencies such as health, law enforcement, justice, social welfare and education.

Guiding principles for promising practices in the provision of services

A growing body of experience indicates that good or promising practices in the provision of services are based on a number of general principles, including to:

- Promote the well-being, physical safety and economic security of victims/survivors and enable women to overcome the multiple consequences of violence to rebuild their lives
- Ensure that victims/survivors have access to appropriate services and that a range of support options are available that take into account the particular access needs of women facing multiple discrimination
- Ensure that service providers are skilled, gender-sensitive, have ongoing training and conduct their work in accordance with clear guidelines, protocols and ethics codes and, where possible, provide female staff
- Maintain the confidentiality and privacy of the victim/survivor
- Cooperate and coordinate with all other services for victims/survivors of violence
- Monitor and evaluate the services provided
- Reject ideologies that excuse or justify men's violence or blame victims
- Empower women to take control of their lives

Forms of service provision

Health services

The health-care system is often the first service to have contact with women victims of violence. It is good practice for the health system to offer a range of interventions to support victims and to ensure that they are not subjected to additional violence within hospitals and health-care facilities. Examples of promising practice in this area include training protocols for health-care providers; integration of victim service centres within the health-care system; and the establishment of referral systems that link relevant sectors, such as health care, counselling, housing, law enforcement services and programmes for perpetrators.

Box 12

One-stop centres

One of the best-known good practices in service provision involves bringing together services in one location, often called the "One-stop centre", an inter-agency unit for victim/survivors of domestic or sexual violence. Such a service was first developed in the largest Government-run general hospital in Malaysia. The victim/survivor is first examined and treated by a doctor and is seen by a counsellor within 24 hours in a separate examination room that protects privacy and confidentiality. If it appears that the victim will be in danger if she returns home, the doctor or counsellor arranges for her to go to an emergency shelter or admits her to the accident and emergency ward for 24 hours. If the patient chooses not to seek shelter, she is encouraged to return to see a social worker at the hospital at a later date. She is also encouraged to make a police report at the police unit based in the hospital. In a case involving severe injury, the police see the patient in the ward to record her statement and start investigations. This model is currently being replicated in much of Asia as well as in other countries, including South Africa.

Sexual assault centres

Victims of sexual violence, including rape, require immediate health care and support and evidence for any resulting legal case also needs to be collected. Physical examinations following sexual violence may be experienced as further violence, or at least as invasive. Lack of timely access to such services can prevent women from getting the evidence needed to bring a rape charge. Protocols and guidelines on forensic examinations in cases of sexual violence are therefore important, as is women's access to such services. Sexual assault centres aim to provide a high standard of comprehensive care to victims of recent sexual assault. Many countries operate hospital-based sexual assault centres or community-based centres near a partner hospital. Some countries, such as Canada, have extensive networks of centres, while others, such as Germany, Switzerland and the United Kingdom, have a number of centres, often in major cities where women's groups or committed medical staff have campaigned to improve local provision.[354]

Hotlines and helplines

Hotlines and helplines provide important access to information and support systems for victims of violence against women and constitute good practice. Such advice lines are now considered a standard component of services in many countries. Because many women are hesitant to seek help, advice lines need to preserve the privacy and confidentiality of their clients and to provide information free of charge. New information and communication technologies expand the potential of such advice lines to provide services in previously deprived locations and in different languages.

The operation of at least one 24-hour national emergency telephone line providing information, advocacy, support and crisis counselling would constitute good practice. Locally appropriate methods of distributing information about the advice line and of ensuring resources for its operation are vital. The National Institute of Women in Costa Rica established a 24-hour toll-free phone line "Break the Silence" in 1997. There was a sharp increase in the number of calls in 2000 and 2001 as a result of publicity about the line and its coordination with the country's emergency number. The hotline 1366 in the Republic of Korea assists and advises victims of violence and is accessible 24 hours a day, with interpretation services for victims of trafficking.[355] The Croatian Government has funded the operating costs for a dedicated national SOS hotline for victims of trafficking.[356]

Shelters

Shelters were originally set up by women's organizations to meet women's need for immediate protection and care when fleeing abusive situations. They have evolved to be much more than "safe houses" and now often provide a range of services. Ensuring that women have access to shelters that meet safety standards to protect them from further violence is good practice. According to the recommendations of an expert group of the Council of Europe, one place in a women's shelter should be provided per 7,500 inhabitants and the minimum standard should be one place per 10,000 inhabitants.[357] The European network, Women Against Violence Europe, has developed quality standards for women's shelters.[358]

While the State may not always be the best provider of such shelters, it is good practice for the State to assist, encourage, finance and cooperate with NGOs in establishing and maintaining them. For example, the First Women's Centre in Kyiv, Ukraine, was established through the coordinated efforts of women's groups and the city administration. This initiative led to a number of shelters being established throughout the country. These shelters work 24 hours a day and offer free services including accommodation for women and their children, medical help, legal consultation, psychological consultation and some social support.[359] Dastak in Lahore, Pakistan, formed by an NGO, provides a halfway house service to women fleeing from their homes because of violence that is open to women and girls of all ages and provides security, legal aid and skills training.[360]

Self-help groups and counselling services

Self-help groups and counselling services are promising, as they provide support for women while respecting their autonomy and encouraging their independent decision-making. Counselling involves professionals working with individual victims/survivors, while self-help groups involve a group of victims/survivors who provide support to each other. For example, Women You Are Not Alone, a self-help group dealing with domestic violence in Costa Rica, works to give women the confidence and support they need to end violent relationships or to renegotiate them. The factors identified as contributing to the success of this group are that women feel empowered by listening to others who have escaped violent situations; they feel understood and appreciated while not being questioned; and they are informed of their rights while being allowed to think for themselves.[361] The Autonomous Women's Centre in Belgrade, provides an example of counselling services for victims of violence. The counsellors at the Centre follow a code of ethics, clear guidelines and protocols and receive ongoing training. They follow three basic principles in providing counselling services: trust women's experience, do not blame women for the violence they have experienced and do not give advice but foster women's self-determination.[362]

Legal services

Women victims/survivors of violence often need legal services to address a variety of issues such as divorce, child custody, child support and maintenance, property settlements, housing, employment and civil suits. The availability of such services, including free legal aid and advice for indigent women, is a promising practice. Legal services may be provided as part of an integrated model of support or by legal aid centres, community legal services or networks of pro bono lawyers. The provision of free legal aid and advice to indigent women is a promising practice. GABRIELA, an NGO in the Philippines, integrates the provision of legal services with counselling, home visits and shelter.[363] While legal services to victims of violence against women are usually provided by civil society organizations, it is good practice for Governments to support such projects, particularly through funding.

Services for victims of trafficking

Victims of trafficking encounter many obstacles in accessing services because they are often afraid of reprisals by trafficking networks; they may lack legal literacy and confidence in legal systems; many fear arrest, legal sanctions and deportation; and they frequently face language barriers.[364] Their immediate needs are protection, medical care, access to legal advice and counselling. If they are repatriated, they require services in their country of origin. Good practice in the provision of services to victims of trafficking requires that these complexities are addressed.

In Bosnia and Herzegovina, the Government provides free legal aid to victims of trafficking and partially finances the shelters run by NGOs for them. An important policy that has emerged from the collaboration between the Government and NGOs is official recognition of the trauma suffered by victims of trafficking who are therefore given 15 days in the shelter before they are interviewed.

In Italy, victims of trafficking can receive residence permits if their life is in danger or if they risk further exploitation. The residence permit allows the trafficking victim to work and requires the victim's participation in an assistance and social reintegration programme, during which the victim can reflect on whether she wishes to report the crime to the police. The trafficked person is provided with medical and psychological assistance, legal advice, training and education opportunities, which are provided through cooperation between NGOs, law enforcement officials and local authorities.

A programme run by an NGO, Reaching Out Romania, provides shelter, counselling, medical, educational and vocational assistance and life skills training support to women and girls trafficked for sexual exploitation. The organization helps trafficked women to find accommodation after leaving the shelter and offers continued counselling services.[365]

Services for victims/survivors of violence against women during and after armed conflict

During and after armed conflict, women in disproportionate numbers may suffer certain forms of violence and they may also be targeted for gender-specific forms of violence. As a result, their physical, psychological and reproductive well-being may be severely compromised. Women have been the targets of sexual violence, including rape, during armed conflict. The consequences of such violence include exposure to sexually transmitted infections, including HIV/AIDS, and unwanted or forced pregnancies. In addition, women who are forcibly displaced or are refugees face a high risk of gender-based violence. The range of services required to assist victims/survivors of violence against women include: comprehensive medical services, including access to safe abortion; counselling; shelter; provision of basic necessities such as food, water and sanitation; and community services and education.

Coordination and multi-agency work

Inter-agency cooperation and coordination in service provision constitutes a good practice, since the creation of services and support for victims and sanctions for perpetrators requires the interlinking of a number of agencies and services. Women victims/survivors often face a range of practical issues, involving criminal and civil law, as well as housing and employment related matters. Many coordinated responses to violence against women, such as the One-stop centres and Duluth model (*see boxes 12 and 13*), integrate various forms of service provision. Singapore uses a "Many Helping Hands" approach to combating violence against women and has developed a manual entitled "Integrated management of family violence cases in Singapore", to map out the protocol, procedures, roles and responsibilities of each partner agency in the network.[366] Greece has in place an integrated programme of action against human trafficking, involving all relevant ministries and a general secretariat for gender equality. The programme includes a permanent forum for exchange of opinions and information between ministries and NGOs.[367]

Box 13
Duluth model of a coordinated community approach to domestic violence

A leading early example of a coordinated community approach to domestic violence was developed in the city of Duluth, Minnesota, United States. The Duluth programme coordinates different aspects of the legal system (including police, criminal court, civil court and probation officers) and forges links between the legal system and resources such as battered women's shelters and advocacy programmes. This approach has been replicated in many countries around the world, including a number of countries throughout Central and Eastern Europe and the former Soviet Union.

Promising practices in prevention

Prevention efforts fall into three categories: primary—stopping violence before it occurs; secondary—an immediate response after violence has occurred to limit its extent and consequences; and tertiary—longer-term care and support for those who have suffered violence.[368] This section focuses on promising practices in primary prevention of violence against women.

Primary prevention requires changing attitudes and challenging stereotypes in society and assisting communities that seek to end the acceptance of violence against women. It also requires women to be empowered both politically and economically, so as to overcome their subordinate position in society. The impact of different prevention measures remains difficult to evaluate. While NGOs pioneered prevention efforts through advocacy, awareness-raising and community mobilization, States have become increasingly active in this area. They have worked to create an enabling and non-discriminatory legal environment, prepare national plans of action and promote public safety, education efforts and media involvement.

Guiding principles of promising practices in prevention

Experience suggests that good or promising practice in the area of primary prevention should be based on a number of guiding principles, including the following:

- Prioritize the prevention of violence against women in all policies and programmes

- Allocate specific resources within all sectors for prevention activities

- Seek political support for sustained long-term investment in prevention

- Develop prevention strategies that address the causes of violence against women, particularly the persistence of gender-based stereotypes

- Outline clear objectives, defining what prevention strategies are seeking to change and how, and put in place a process of monitoring and evaluation

- Ensure that the perspectives and voices of women, particularly victims/survivors, are central to the development of prevention strategies

- Work with a cross-section of stakeholders, including government bodies, NGOs, workers' and employers' organizations and local community leaders, to build inclusive and effective strategies

- Engage men and boys proactively in strategy development and implementation for the prevention of male violence against women

- Highlight the fact that violence against women is unacceptable and its elimination is a public responsibility

- Promote women's safety, including by altering physical environments where necessary
- Ensure that prevention efforts are holistic, take into account multiple discrimination and connect wherever possible with other key issues for women, such as HIV/AIDS

Prevention strategies

Advocacy and campaigns

Advocacy efforts, especially campaigns to expose and convey the unacceptability of violence against women, continue to be instrumental in stimulating change and are good practice. They enhance women's awareness of their rights and of available remedies and services. While such campaigns began as initiatives of the women's movement, many Governments now regularly include them in awareness-raising and prevention strategies. Campaigns have used different means, including theatre, demonstrations, vigils, print, radio, television and the Internet.

The Scottish zero tolerance campaign is an example of a sustained national campaign that ran over five years, linking rape, sexual harassment, domestic violence and child sexual abuse. The campaign was undertaken by an NGO and supported by the State. This project drew on graphic design and social marketing techniques, using inviting images alongside uncompromising slogans, such as "No man has the right", which were displayed on billboards, on buses and in other public places. Each phase of the campaign was linked to research and accompanied by work on the "three p's"—provision, protection and prevention.

The Australian Government ran a campaign in 2004 to condemn domestic and sexual violence. This campaign comprised television, radio, cinema and magazine commercials, a household information booklet, a schools kit, a website and a nationwide 24-hour hotline.[369] The Danish Government similarly ran a comprehensive nationwide campaign on the theme "Stop the violence against women: break the silence" in 2003. The campaign was launched in Danish, English, Arabic, Turkish and Somali and aimed to break the taboo surrounding violence against women and to inform women about their rights and options.[370]

The Tanzania Media Women's Association, an NGO, ran a comprehensive media campaign in 1998 to promote the enactment of the Sexual Offences Special Provision Act, a law to criminalize female genital mutilation/cutting. The campaign used social and journalistic surveys, radio programmes, television and multi-media news and features. It involved interaction between NGOs, media practitioners and theatre artists. It produced education materials, information kits, an international appeal/manifesto and a website (www.stopfgm.org) in English, French and Arabic.[371]

An NGO global campaign entitled "16 Days of activism against gender-based violence against women", has been held every year since 1991 between 25 November and 10 December. It has involved groups in almost every country in the world. The campaign develops both a global action kit and local materials to raise awareness of violence against women and to link it to other events and issues, such as HIV/AIDS. The campaign also provides a worldwide forum for organizers to develop and share strategies. In 2005, activities took place in some 130 countries, involving different levels and sectors of Government, parts of the United Nations system and international and local NGOs. The "16 Days of activism" campaign exemplifies government involvement in a campaign initiated by civil society, as well as effective and creative use of information and communications technologies.[372]

Community mobilization

Mobilization strategies at the community level can contribute to the prevention of violence against women.[373] Good practice in community mobilization involves a participatory process and the engagement of all levels of society, including local government representatives, community leaders, NGOs and women's groups.

The "Raising voices" programme in Kampala is a multisectoral community-level prevention effort seeking to promote change through reduced tolerance of violence against women by local councils, police and the community at large.[374] In the Deir El Barsha in the Minya governate in upper Egypt, where female genital mutilation/cutting was widely practised, NGOs used community mobilization to inform local and religious leaders of the adverse effects of the practice. These leaders reached out to families within their areas of influence. Villagers drew up a social contract in which everyone in the village committed to ending the practice: parents agreed not to subject their daughters to female genital mutilation/cutting, young men committed to marry uncircumcised girls and those who performed female genital mutilation/cutting agreed to end their work.[375]

Working with men

The struggle to transform gender relations and to eliminate violence against women cannot be successful without the involvement of men. There are promising examples of coalitions in which men address the need to end community acquiescence in violence against women and support women's leadership roles. Strategies to engage men in the prevention of violence against women have included work to raise awareness of the issue with organized groups—such as the military, trade unions, sports teams and the police—as well as campaigns that utilize positive male role models to oppose violence against women.

The White Ribbon Campaign encourages men and boys to wear white ribbons on November 25—the International Day for the Elimination of Violence against Women—as a personal pledge never to commit, condone or remain silent about violence against women.[376] The campaign has developed educational materials and action kits aimed at transforming men's attitudes that have been distributed to schools, universities, corporations and labour unions. Since its inception in Canada in 1991, the White Ribbon Campaign has spread to 47 countries in Africa, Asia, Europe, Latin America and the Pacific.[377]

The mayor of a town in Honduras engaged men's help in educating the community on violence against women and linked training for men on the issue of violence against women to the purchase of new football equipment. Many men became actively involved in the campaign and men's football teams began to carry placards promoting respect for women's human rights before each game and during half-time.[378] The New South Wales state government in Australia also used well-known male athletes in its community education campaign "Violence against women: it's against all the rules" aimed at men aged 21 to 29.[379]

Using the news media and information technology

Training and sensitization of journalists and other media personnel who report on violence against women is a promising practice as it can enhance the quality of reporting and contribute to increased awareness and understanding of the causes and consequences of violence against women among the general public. In Nepal, women journalists formed a communication group to monitor domestic violence reported in newspapers and to provide training to people in the media on violence against women, encouraging them to report cases of violence in a victim-sensitive manner.

The creative use of popular media to reach wider audiences is also a promising practice. An example is a music video made by an Indian women's human rights group, Breakthrough, which addressed domestic violence and empowerment of the survivor. It reached more than 26 million households throughout India, and reached the top 10 in the country's music charts.[380]

Use of new information and communications technologies such as cell phones and the Internet can be good practice to disseminate information widely and allow interaction between stakeholders in various locations. The website www.stopfgm.org, referred to above, exemplifies the use of the Internet as an international platform to raise awareness, analyse and disseminate information and share good practices on the elimination of female genital mutilation/cutting.

Promoting public safety

It is good practice to make the physical environment safer for women and community safety audits have been used to identify dangerous locations, discuss women's fears and obtain women's recommendations for improving their safety. Prevention of violence against women should be an explicit element in urban and rural planning and in the design of buildings and residential dwellings. Improving the safety of public transport and routes travelled by women, such as to schools and educational institutions or to wells, fields and factories, is part of prevention work. The "Safer cities" initiative in the United Republic of Tanzania, for example, builds the capacity of local authorities to address issues of urban insecurity in partnership with local communities and other stakeholders. Safety audits were conducted under this initiative in which women participated in "exploratory walkabouts" and identified unsafe areas and recommended solutions for action by appropriate authorities.[381] Initiatives to enhance the safety of women living in refugee camps to gather firewood have also been implemented.

Education and capacity-building

The formal education system can be used as a key site for raising awareness about violence against women and challenging and eradicating gender stereotypes. Promising practices in this area include eliminating gender-based stereotypes in educational curricula; providing gender-sensitivity training for teachers; creating a school environment that rejects violence; and offering specialized courses on human rights, including women's rights.

Other prevention strategies

There are many other examples of promising efforts and interventions focused on prevention. NGOs have used hearings and tribunals in which victims/survivors of violence against women tell their stories, exposing the realities of such violence and calling for attention to measures for prevention. Women's rights advocates have lobbied Governments and parliamentarians to pursue prevention strategies more vigorously. Litigation in cases involving violence against women has been used to expose gaps in protection and remedies and the need for more prevention. Prevention strategies based on working with perpetrators towards gender-equitable relationships and in training community members in basic conflict resolution skills have also been developed. Sharing experiences and lessons, including across borders, has enhanced knowledge about prevention and should be encouraged and supported.

Challenges for implementation

Despite the progress of recent decades and the emergence of promising practices in many areas, the struggle to eliminate violence against women continues to face multiple challenges. At the same time, some good practices may encounter drawbacks in application, which need to be addressed. For example, while specialized procedures may be established for the purpose of expedited reporting, investigation and prosecution of cases of violence against women, in practice such procedures may be marginalized and not receive the support and resources they need to function effectively. They may at the same time result in mainstream mechanisms of justice, including the police and courts, not developing the required expertise for handling violence against women cases professionally and effectively. Alternative dispute resolution mechanisms likewise have to be examined critically for their appropriateness and the consequences of moving responsibility for the issue of violence against women out of the mainstream justice system, especially if such alternative mechanisms place high priority on community cohesion or family reputation rather than the rights of victims.

While women's agency and empowerment are crucial dimensions of good practices, it is not always clear how these goals can be most effectively pursued. For example, so-called no-drop policies, under which the State undertakes an investigation and prosecution even if the victim/survivor wishes to drop the case. The imposition of appropriate punishments for acts of violence against women, including prison terms, may also function as a disincentive for victims/survivors to report cases when they do not want their abusive partner to be prosecuted or incarcerated for various reasons.

Inconsistent efforts and inadequate resources indicating a lack of political will

State efforts to address violence against women are neither consistent nor sustained. Many specific shortcomings in efforts to eliminate violence against women at the national level have been identified by the human rights treaty bodies, as outlined in section VI. While the reasons for such a lack of systematic effort may vary, violence against women is generally not treated as seriously as other forms of crime or human rights abuse. The level of investment and resources allocated to legal and support services, let alone prevention, remains minimal compared with many other issues.

Lack of a comprehensive and integrated approach

While there is wide agreement that comprehensive and coordinated multisectoral efforts by multiple stakeholders are necessary to eliminate violence against women, such efforts are rarely forthcoming on a large scale or in a sustained manner. Although models of comprehensive integrated approaches have been developed, these have been sporadically implemented and replication has not always been successful, owing to the absence of vital components, including resources.

Lack of funding

Legal, service and prevention efforts to address violence against women require a sustained funding stream. The main sources of funding are States and donors. State funding for such initiatives has historically been inadequate. Funding from donors is often project-driven, not sustained and sometimes not in line with the aspirations of women's groups working on these issues. To ensure viability and sustainability, initiatives on violence against women require funding from the general national budget and not only from specialized funds.

Failure to end impunity

Although efforts to reform criminal justice systems are ongoing, including the enactment of new laws and more effective implementation of legislation, perpetrators of violence against women continue to enjoy impunity. Ensuring that perpetrators are brought to justice is more important than increasing the penalties for violence against women. In fact, demanding draconian sentences and sanctions may have the unintended consequence of decreasing reporting and convictions. At the same time, women lose faith in justice systems where sentences are minimal and fail to offer them any protection.

The intersection of multiple forms of discrimination

The intersection of male dominance with race, ethnicity, age, caste, religion, culture, language, sexual orientation, migrant and refugee status and disability—frequently termed "intersectionality"—operates at many levels in relation to violence against women. Multiple discrimination shapes the forms of violence that a woman experiences. It makes some women more likely to be targeted for certain forms of violence because they have less social status than other women and because perpetrators know such women have fewer options for seeking assistance or reporting.

Lack of evaluation

While research on interventions has expanded considerably, the ability to demonstrate "what works" continues to be limited. Insufficient resources have been devoted to developing methodologies that can trace the subtle and profound changes necessary to end violence against women. Ongoing dialogue between State agencies, NGOs and researchers could contribute to developing and refining new measurements appropriate for various levels of analysis.■

VIII. CONCLUSION AND RECOMMENDATIONS

Conclusion

As this study has shown, violence against women is a widespread and serious problem that affects the lives of countless women and is an obstacle to the achievement of equality, development and peace in all continents. It endangers women's lives and impedes the full development of women's capabilities. It obstructs the exercise of their rights as citizens; it harms families and communities and reinforces other forms of violence throughout societies, often with deadly consequences.

Violence against women is a violation of human rights, rooted in historically unequal power relations between men and women and the systemic discrimination against women that pervades both the public and private spheres. The broad context from which it emerges includes disparities of power in the form of patriarchy, sociocultural norms and practices that perpetuate gender-based discrimination and economic inequalities. Its scope and prevalence reflect the degree and persistence of gender-based discrimination that women face, which is often compounded by other systems of domination. Violence against women must therefore be addressed in the context of seeking to end all forms of discrimination, to advance gender equality and the empowerment of women and to create a world in which all women enjoy all their human rights.

This study outlines many forms and manifestations of violence against women in a wide range of settings, including the family, the community, State custody and institutions, armed conflict and refugee and internally displaced persons situations. Such violence constitutes a continuum across the lifespan of women, it cuts across both the public and the private sphere and one form of violence often reinforces another. Violence against women often takes a direct physical form, but can also be psychological abuse and economic deprivation. Despite the growing acknowledgment of the multiple forms and manifestations of violence against women, comprehensive data to establish the scope and magnitude of the various forms of such violence remains inadequate.

While violence against women is universal and present in every society and culture, it takes different forms and is experienced differently. The forms of violence to which women are subjected and the ways in which they experience this violence are often shaped by the intersection of gender with other factors such as race, ethnicity, class, age, sexual orientation, disability, nationality, legal status, religion and culture. Therefore diverse strategies that take these intersecting factors into account are required in order to eradicate violence against all women.

Over the past two decades, there has been significant progress in elaborating and agreeing on international standards and norms to address violence against women. These form a baseline of commitment by States and other stakeholders, including the United Nations system, to work to end violence against women. States' responsibility and obligations to address violence against women are concrete and clear and encompass violence committed both by State agents and non-State actors. States have a duty to prevent acts of violence against women; to investigate and prosecute such acts when they occur and punish perpetrators; and to provide remedies and redress to those against whom acts of violence have been committed.

To an unacceptable extent, these obligations are not being met. Impunity for violence against women compounds the effects of such violence as a mechanism of male control over women. When the State fails to hold the perpetrators of violence accountable and society explicitly or tacitly condones such violence, impunity not only encourages further abuses, it also gives the message that male violence against women is acceptable or normal. The result of such impunity is not solely the denial of justice to the individual victims/survivors, but also the reinforcement of prevailing gender relations and replication of inequalities that affect other women and girls as well.

There is a significant and unacceptable gap between the international standards on violence against women and the concrete commitment of political capital and resources to implement these standards. The specificities of the State's obligations need to be clarified in the diverse contexts in which violence against women occurs. Varying circumstances and constraints allow for different actions to be taken by individual States, but do not excuse State inaction.

The State has a responsibility for the prevention, punishment and elimination of violence against women that it cannot relegate to other actors. However, there are significant advantages to engaging in partnerships with NGOs and other actors in civil society and the private sector, especially since women's organizations often pilot programmes that Governments can support and replicate or institutionalize. Further, the development of State strategies to address violence should be based on women's experiences and requires their involvement.

The women's movement has been instrumental in identifying a wide range of ways in which women experience violence and bringing these to national and global attention. However, any enumeration of forms of violence at any given time cannot be exhaustive, as male violence against women continues to change, reflecting social, economic and political dynamics. New technologies, such as the Internet, or new circumstances such as free trade zones, can lead to new forms of violence against women. States must be ready to address new forms of violence against women as they appear and are identified.

Violence against women is complex and diverse in its manifestations. This very diversity demonstrates that it is not immutable or inevitable. The enabling conditions for violence against women are socially produced and therefore the processes by which they are produced can be altered. With the necessary political will and resources dedicated to eradicating it and to ensuring that women can enjoy all their human rights, violence against women can be seriously reduced and eventually eliminated. Securing gender equality and ending violence against women must not be treated as optional or marginal tasks. A coordinated, cross-cutting and multisectoral response is required to address violence against women. Strong institutional mechanisms at local, national, regional and international levels are needed to ensure action, coordination, monitoring and accountability.

Continuing pervasive violence against women across the globe fuels cultures of violence and undermines progress towards the goals of human rights, development and peace. There is much at stake for all of humanity in the effort to end violence against women. The time has come for all nations and peoples to make this a local, national, regional and global priority.

End impunity and take action
to address violence against women

Detailed recommendations for action on violence against women have been developed in intergovernmental agreements such as the Beijing Declaration and Platform for Action and in reports, studies and guidelines by United Nations bodies, agencies and mechanisms, academics and NGOs. However, significant gaps remain in their effective implementation. The present recommendations complement existing ones and aim to accelerate implementation of these existing standards, norms and commitments.[382]

The present recommendations are limited to six key areas for action at the national level. Concrete recommendations are also directed at both the intergovernmental level and the United Nations system. They highlight, in particular, the role of the General Assembly in ensuring that meaningful follow-up and implementation is undertaken by different stakeholders. Member States and the international community must acknowledge the devastating impact any further delay in taking these limited but critical measures will have on women, their families and their communities. Together, these recommendations constitute a clear strategy for Member States and the United Nations system to make measurable progress in preventing and eliminating violence against women.

Recommendations at the national level

The following strategic recommendations arising from this study are key to moving the agenda for the elimination of violence against women forward. These recommendations are interrelated and all are crucial for an effective, systematic and comprehensive approach to end violence against women.

Secure gender equality and protect women's human rights

Violence against women is both a cause and a consequence of discrimination against women and of their inequality and subordination. States have an obligation to respect, protect, promote and fulfil all human rights, including the right of women to be free from discrimination. Failure to do so results in and exacerbates violence against women.

Therefore, it is recommended that States:

- Ensure that all human rights and fundamental freedoms are respected, protected and fulfilled

- Ratify without reservations all human rights treaties, including, in particular, the Convention on the Elimination of All Forms of Discrimination against Women and its Optional Protocol

- Ensure that women know their rights and are empowered to demand and exercise them

- Educate men and women, boys and girls about women's human rights and their responsibility to respect the rights of others

- Ensure that women have access to justice and equal protection of the law and that perpetrators of violence against women do not enjoy impunity

- Recognize and protect women's right to control their bodies and their sexuality

- Secure women's rights to inheritance, property, housing and social security, among the range of economic and social rights

- Utilize gender impact assessments to ensure that social and economic policies, including development planning, do not perpetuate or exacerbate violence against women and, instead, actively support the prevention and elimination of violence against women

- Respond to different women's experiences of violence, as such experiences are shaped by the intersection of gender with other factors, such as race, ethnicity, class, age, HIV status, sexual orientation, disability, nationality, legal status, religion and culture

Exercise leadership to end violence against women

Leadership to end all violence against women and advocacy in this regard are critical at all levels (local, national, regional and international) and by all sectors (including State actors, opinion makers, business leaders, civil society organizations and community leaders).

Ending impunity and ensuring accountability for violence against women are crucial actions for preventing and reducing such violence and are visible expressions by States of their commitment to take action.

Accordingly, it is recommended that:

- States speak out forcefully on the urgent need to end violence against women and ensure public accountability for all instances of violence, hold up to public scrutiny and eliminate those institutional and cultural attitudes that foster, justify, or tolerate it

- States do not commit acts of violence against women, ensure that no State agents commit such acts, including by taking punitive or disciplinary action against any State agent who does so, prevent violence against women by non-State actors, prosecute and punish all perpetrators and provide remedies and redress to victims

- Local community leaders and opinion makers (including in schools, religious and traditional institutions, community organizations, trade unions, businesses and the media) play a key role in generating political will and sustained action to end community tolerance of, and complicity in, male violence against women

- Men and boys be encouraged to speak out strongly against violence against women and to stop protecting perpetrators or condoning their violence

- Women providing leadership on ending violence against women at all levels, and especially in grassroots women's organizations, be recognized and allowed to carry out their work unhindered, as well as actively supported in their efforts

Close the gaps between international standards and national laws, policies and practices

International standards and norms are not yet sufficiently implemented in practice. Impunity for violence against women (by both State and non-State actors) results from the failure to meet international standards through substantial national and local action and implementation.

Accordingly, it is recommended that States:

- Bring national laws, policies and practices into compliance with international commitments

- Follow-up on and implement the recommendations that emanate from periodic reviews of their reports and communications and inquiry procedures, as applicable, by human rights treaty bodies, in particular those of the Committee on the Elimination of Discrimination against Women

- Remove all laws that discriminate against women; review and revise all State policies and practices to ensure that they do not discriminate against women; and ensure that provisions of multiple legal systems, where they exist, comply with international human rights standards, including the principle of non-discrimination

- Ensure that legislation is in place that adequately addresses all forms of violence against women

- Act with due diligence to prevent violence against women; to investigate such violence; to prosecute and punish perpetrators, whether they are State or non-State actors; and to provide access to redress for victims

- Take positive measures to address structural causes of violence against women and to strengthen prevention efforts that address discriminatory practices and social norms

- Institute plans of action that are regularly monitored and updated by Governments in consultation with civil society, in particular, NGOs and women's groups and networks

- Promote victims/survivors' knowledge of their rights and remedies available to them and their capacity to claim them through effective access to justice

- Promote the competence of all personnel in the legal and criminal justice, health and education systems to meet the needs and secure the rights of victims/survivors through professional education, training and other capacity-building programmes

- Guarantee appropriate support for women victims/survivors through adequate and accessible services that foster women's safety and agency

- Protect women in conflict, post-conflict and refugee and internally displaced persons settings where women are particularly targeted for violence and their ability to seek and receive redress is restricted and adopt a gender-sensitive approach to the granting of asylum

- Address stereotypical attitudes and behaviours that contribute to male violence against women, working specifically with men and boys, and encourage other stakeholders to implement measures as part of preventing violence against women

- Review and strengthen their work with perpetrators and, in particular, assess the impact of rehabilitation programmes with a view to broadening available strategies for preventing violence against women

Strengthen the knowledge base on all forms of violence against women to inform policy and strategy development

There remains a dearth of reliable information about the scope and extent of violence against women, especially some of its forms. Data that assesses and evaluates what policies and practices are most effective in preventing and addressing such violence is particularly scarce. Limited availability of data, however, does not diminish State responsibility for addressing violence against women.

Accordingly, it is recommended that States:

- Take responsibility for the systematic collection and analysis of data. They should carry out this work themselves or in partnership with other actors. This may include supporting and facilitating the work of NGOs, academics and others engaged in such activities

- Ensure that data is disaggregated, not only by sex, but also by other factors such as race, age and disability, as appropriate

- Ensure that national statistical offices and other bodies involved in the collection of data on violence against women receive the necessary training for undertaking this work

- Ensure that the information from the data collection and analysis is made widely available to the public and acted upon as appropriate

- Use internationally comparable measurements about the scope, prevalence and incidence of all forms and manifestations of violence against women in their data collection efforts, to allow monitoring of their progress in meeting obligations to address violence against women

It is also necessary that:

- Data be collected in a way that respects confidentiality and women's human rights and does not jeopardize women's safety

- Evaluative data on promising practices be developed and utilized in order to facilitate the replication, scaling up and institutionalization of the most effective interventions

- Data on violence against women be included in national and international data collection efforts, including those undertaken in conjunction with policy planning and implementation processes for poverty reduction strategies and human rights monitoring. National statistical offices have a key role to play in these efforts

- Methodologies for measuring the economic and developmental costs of violence against women for victims/survivors, households and society in different settings be enhanced and further developed

Build and sustain strong multisectoral strategies, coordinated nationally and locally

Work to end violence against women should go beyond ad hoc, single-sector or single-issue responses to a comprehensive, systematic and sustained approach that is adequately supported and facilitated by strong dedicated and permanent institutional mechanisms. This should involve such government sectors as justice, health, housing and education as well as defence, finance, foreign affairs, agriculture and labour. Coordination among different sectors and levels is critical in assisting women who survive violence to access effective legal, health and social services, as well as enhancing prevention work.

Accordingly, it is recommended that States:

- Exercise their responsibility for coordination across all national and local government sectors as a key component in building sustainable strategies to end violence against women

- Create strong institutional mechanisms at local, regional and national levels to ensure action, coordination, monitoring and accountability

- Integrate efforts to prevent and reduce male violence against women into a wide range of programme areas such as HIV/AIDS, reproductive health, urban planning, immigration, poverty reduction, development, conflict, post-conflict and refugee situations and humanitarian relief

- Integrate a comprehensive understanding of the causes and consequences of violence against women into appropriate education and training curricula at all levels, including, among others, in the professional education of health workers, teachers, law enforcement personnel and social workers

Allocate adequate resources and funding

Violence against women impoverishes individuals, families, communities and countries. The social, political and economic costs of allowing it to continue unabated are great and call for a commensurate investment in women's security. Such an effort requires increased political will expressed through a much greater commitment of financial and human resources.

Accordingly, it is recommended that States:

- Increase funding to provide adequate services and access to justice and redress to victims/survivors

- Assess budgets at national and local levels from a gender perspective and correct imbalances in order to ensure a more equitable allocation of resources to eliminating discrimination and violence against women

- Fund work on violence against women from national budgets

- Secure additional resources from specialized funds and donors for programmes to address violence against women, particularly the least developed countries and countries in or emerging from conflict

It is also necessary that States, donors and international organizations:

- Allocate significant resources to eliminate discrimination against women, promote gender equality and prevent and redress all forms and manifestations of violence against women

- Provide resources to evaluate and monitor innovative programming by Governments and NGOs and support scaling up of the most promising practices and successful pilot projects

Recommendations at the international level

Since the Fourth World Conference on Women, increased attention has been given to violence against women throughout the United Nations system, both in intergovernmental and expert bodies, as well as in the entities of the United Nations system.

These efforts have yet to produce a comprehensive, systematic, well-coordinated and properly resourced response. As a result, there is limited implementation of commitments, norms and standards. Moreover, emerging concerns, such as the linkages between violence against women and other issues, new forms of violence against women or new situations leading to violence against women, also need to be addressed. There is some targeted attention to violence against women in certain areas, but work on violence against women is yet to become an integral part in all policies, programmes and action.

Consequently, violence against women has not received the visibility and prominence required to enable significant change. A more cohesive and strategic approach is needed to tackle the challenges outlined in this study and addressed in the six strategic areas of recommendations above. Such an approach requires the enhanced collaboration of all actors, including Governments, the international community and civil society.

The present section addresses the need for a more systematic and comprehensive focus on violence against women within the United Nations system. The important initiative of the General Assembly in calling for this study needs to be followed by resolve at all levels for concrete action to prevent and eliminate violence against women.

A stronger, more consistent and visible leadership role by intergovernmental bodies and the entities of the United Nations system is necessary, demonstrated by political will, greater prominence on the international agenda, sustained action and more significant allocation of resources to strengthen implementation of the normative and policy framework for addressing violence against women.

Intergovernmental level

It is recommended that intergovernmental bodies strengthen accountability for action on violence against women with a view to accelerating implementation of commitments, norms and standards, on violence against women, nationally, regionally and internationally.

In particular, it is recommended that:

- The General Assembly consider annually the question of violence against women, based on one report of the Secretary-General. Such consideration should build on and complement the targeted and sector-specific work undertaken on violence against women by other intergovernmental bodies. While addressing violence against women holistically, the General Assembly should also place emphasis on new and emerging concerns, including linkages between violence against women and other issues such as HIV/AIDS, poverty eradication, food security, peace and security, humanitarian responses, health, or crime prevention

- The Security Council intensify efforts to address gender-based violence against women and consistently monitor measures taken within the framework of the implementation of Security Council resolution 1325 (2000) on women and peace and security. Towards this end, the Security Council should consider establishing a dedicated monitoring mechanism to increase the effectiveness of the Council's contribution to preventing and redressing violence against women in armed conflict

- Intergovernmental bodies, including the Peacebuilding Commission, the Human Rights Council, the Economic and Social Council and its functional commissions, especially the Commission on the Status of Women, the Commission on Crime Prevention and Criminal Justice and the Statistics Commission, discuss, by 2008, the question of violence against women in all its forms and manifestations in relation to their mandates, and set priorities for addressing this issue in their future efforts and work programmes. Intergovernmental bodies should also identify and address gaps in the international policy and normative framework pertaining to violence against women within their respective areas of competence

- The Human Rights Council reaffirms the mandate of the Special Rapporteur on violence against women, its causes and consequences, which has been critical to the expansion of work on violence against women and, in coordination with the Commission on the Status of Women, requests the Special Rapporteur to report annually to both the Human Rights Council and the Commission on the Status of Women in its role as a central intergovernmental body in the follow-up to and implementation of the Beijing Declaration and Platform for Action

- The General Assembly strengthens the Office of the Special Adviser to the Secretary-General on Gender Issues and Advancement of Women as a mechanism to enhance visibility and strengthen coordination and advocacy for the elimination of violence against women at the international and regional level. Such efforts should in particular aim to enhance coordination of a system-wide approach, including at country level. Responsibility for such coordination should be located at the level of the Chief Executives Board for Coordination

United Nations system

Coordination within the United Nations system and institutional support

In order to maximize efficient and effective use of existing structures and resources and to ensure coherence and coordination, it is recommended that the following measures be taken:

- Entities of the United Nations system clearly identify how violence against women affects the effective implementation of their mandates and strengthen their response to such violence. They should in particular enhance efforts that respond to the cross-cutting nature of violence against women and link those efforts with their work on issues such as HIV/AIDS, poverty eradication, food security, peace and security, humanitarian responses, health, education, legal and judicial reform or crime prevention

- The Special Adviser to the Secretary-General on Gender Issues and Advancement of Women, through the Inter-Agency Network on Women and Gender Equality, leads an enhanced system-wide coordination of this work in order to ensure greater visibility, consistency, effective action, monitoring, reporting and accountability and reports thereon to the High-level Committees on Programme and Management and, ultimately, the Chief Executives Board for Coordination. The task force on violence against women set up by the Network supports the Special Adviser in this effort

- The Special Adviser to the Secretary-General on Gender Issues and Advancement of Women, UNIFEM as the Trust Fund manager and the task force on violence against women of the Inter-Agency Network on Women and Gender Equality, consider ways and means for enhancing the effectiveness of the United Nations Trust Fund to End Violence against Women as a system-wide mechanism for preventing and redressing violence against women and for increasing feedback of lessons learned from supported projects into the system-wide policy and normative work on violence against women

Collection of data, and research

The United Nations system has a significant role to play in strengthening the capacity of countries to collect, process and disseminate data on male violence against women and to use such data as a basis for legislative, policy and programme development.

As a priority, the United Nations system should undertake to:

- Provide technical support to countries and promote existing methodologies and good practices to ensure that existing standards of excellence on data collection are met

- Support the development of unified methods and standards for data collection on all forms of violence against women that are under-documented

- Support evaluation research and impact analysis of interventions to prevent and redress violence against women

- Develop common indicators for evaluating and monitoring State compliance with international agreements

- Build capacity of national statistical offices, women's national machineries, international and national research institutions and NGOs and strengthen links between them

- Link efforts to collect data on violence against women to existing and ongoing data collection efforts, including planning processes for poverty reduction strategies and human rights monitoring

- Establish a coordinated and easily accessible United Nations database within the Department of Economic and Social Affairs, involving in particular the Division for the Advancement of Women and developed in collaboration with the Statistics Division of the Department of Economic and Social Affairs, the regional commissions and all other relevant parts of the United Nations system on statistics, legislation, training models, good practices, ethical guidelines and other resources regarding all forms and manifestations of violence against women

- Convene a United Nations working group to develop and propose a set of international indicators for assessing the scope, prevalence and incidence of violence against women, monitoring progress in addressing such violence and assessing the impact of different measures and interventions. This work should build on existing proposals for indicators on violence against women, as well as on the work of the Special Rapporteur on violence against women, its causes and consequences, called for in resolution 2004/46 of the Commission on Human Rights

**Operational activities at the country level,
including in the framework of humanitarian assistance
and peacekeeping missions**

It is recommended that the following measures be taken:

- United Nations Resident Coordinators take a leadership role in advocating for an effective and comprehensive response to violence against women at the national level and systematically support Governments and other actors in their actions to prevent and eliminate violence against women

- United Nations country teams support development of (when applicable), and full implementation, of comprehensive national actions plans on violence against women that include national awareness-raising campaigns and place emphasis on strengthening knowledge of rights and availability of services and on changing gender-based stereotypical norms and attitudes that condone and perpetuate male violence against women

- United Nations country teams give greater priority to prevent and respond to violence against women, including through a more coordinated system-wide approach to programming and through collaboration with women's groups and civil society

- The capacity of United Nations country teams to deal with violence against women be strengthened, including through training

- Special Representatives of the Secretary-General give priority attention to violence against women within their mandates in peacekeeping and peacebuilding missions

Resources

It is recommended that the following measures be undertaken:

- The resources allocated throughout the United Nations system to address violence against women be increased significantly

- Entities of the United Nations system and all other donors provide increased resources for the implementation of comprehensive national action plans aimed at preventing and eliminating violence against women, particularly in the least developed countries and in countries emerging from conflict

- Entities of the United Nations system allocate an increased share of the resources devoted to issues such as poverty reduction, HIV/AIDS and peacekeeping for the specific purpose of prevention and elimination of violence against women, to identify and address the intersection with violence against women

- States, donors and international organizations increase significantly the financial support for work on violence against women in United Nations agencies and programmes, including to the United Nations Trust Fund to End Violence against Women ■

NOTES

[1] See E/CN.4/2003/75, executive summary.

[2] Convention for the Suppression of the Traffic in Persons and of the Exploitation of the Prostitution of Others (1949); *Women Go Global: The United Nations and the International Women's Movement*, 1945-2000, CD-ROM (United Nations publication, Sales No. E.01.IV.1).

[3] See Sen, P., "Successes and Challenges: Understanding the Global Movement to End Violence Against Women in Global Civil Society", Kaldor, M., Anheier, H. and Glasius, M., eds. (London, Centre for the Study of Global Governance, 2003); Reilly, N. ed., *Without Reservation: The Beijing Tribunal on Accountability for Women's Human Rights* (New Jersey, Center for Women's Global Leadership, 1996); and Jain, D., *Women, Development, and the UN: A Sixty Year Quest for Equality and Justice* (Bloomington, Indiana University Press, 2005).

[4] *Report of the World Conference of the International Women's Year*, Mexico City, 19 June-2 July 1975 (United Nations publication, Sales No. E.76.IV.1).

[5] Russell, D. and Van de Ven, N., *Crimes against women: The proceedings of the International Tribunal* (East Palo Alto, Frog in the Well Press, 1984).

[6] *Report of the World Conference of the United Nations Decade for Women: Equality, Development and Peace*, Copenhagen, 14-30 July 1980 (United Nations publication, Sales No. E.80.IV.3 and corrigendum).

[7] See Antrobus, P., *The Global Women's Movement: Origins, Issues and Strategies* (London, Zed Books, 2004); and Bunch, C., *Passionate Politics* (New York, St. Martins Press, 1987).

[8] *Report of the World Conference to Review and Appraise the Achievement of the United Nations Decade for Women: Equality, Development and Peace*, Nairobi, 15-26 July 1985 (United Nations publication, Sales No. E.85.IV.10).

[9] *Sixth United Nations Congress on the Prevention of Crime and Treatment of Offenders*, Caracas, 25 August–5 September 1980 (United Nations publication, Sales No. E.81.IV.4); *Seventh United Nations Congress on the Prevention of Crime and Treatment of Offenders*, Milan, 26 August-6 September 1985 (United Nations publication, Sales No. E.86.IV.1).

[10] *Violence against women in the family*, New York, 1989 (United Nations publication, Sales No. E.89.IV.5).

[11] See Bunch, C. and Reilly, N., *Demanding Accountability: The Global Campaign and Vienna Tribunal for Women's Human Rights* (New Jersey, Center for Women's Global Leadership/ UNIFEM, 1994).

[12] General Assembly resolution 34/180.

[13] See A/44/38.

[14] See A/47/38, 1992.

[15] General Assembly resolution 48/104.

[16] Ibid, preamble.

[17] See A/CONF.157/23, para 18.

[18] The mandate of the Special Rapporteur on violence against women, its causes and consequences, was established by the Commission on Human Rights in 1994 (Commission on Human Rights resolution 1994/45) and was extended in 1997, 2000 and 2003 (Commission on Human Rights resolutions 1997/44, 2000/45 and 2003/45).

[19] *Report of the Fourth World Conference on Women*, Beijing, 4-15 September 1995 (United Nations publication, Sales No. E.96.IV.13).

[20] See General Assembly resolution S-23/3, annex, para. 13.

[21] Security Council resolution 1325 (2000).

[22] Coomaraswamy, R., "The varied contours of violence against women in South Asia", paper presented at the Fifth South Asia Regional Ministerial Conference, Celebrating Beijing + 10, Islamabad, Pakistan, 3-5 May 2005.

[23] See note 11, p. 117.

[24] See Committee on the Elimination of Discrimination against Women general recommendation No. 19; Human Rights Committee, general comment 28; and Committee on Economic, Social and Cultural Rights general comment 16, in: HRI/GEN/1/Rev. 8.

[25] See Committee on the Elimination of Discrimination against Women general recommendation No. 19; Committee on the Elimination of Racial Discrimination, general recommendation 25. See note 24.

[26] General Assembly resolutions 60/139, 59/167, 59/166, 59/165, 58/147 and Commission on Human Rights resolutions 2005/41 and 2001/49.

[27] General Assembly resolution 54/134.

[28] *Report of the International Conference on Population and Development*, Cairo, 5-13 September 1994 (United Nations publication, Sales No. 95.XIII.18), para. 4.4 (e).

[29] General Assembly resolution 55/2.

[30] General Assembly resolution 60/1, para. 58. United Nations Millennium Project, *Taking Action: Achieving Gender Equality and Empowering Women*, Task Force on Education and Gender Equality (London, Earthscan, 2005).

[31] Division for the Advancement of Women, *Final report of the workshop on violence against women for entities of the United Nations system*, New York, 5–7 December 2005, available at http://www.un.org/womenwatch/daw/vaw, and Division for the Advancement of Women, *Preventing and eliminating violence against women: An inventory of United Nations system activities on violence against women*.

[32] Resolution adopted at the 114th Assembly of the Inter-Parliamentary Union, Nairobi, 12 May 2006.

[33] E/CN.6/2000/2 and E/CN.6/2005/2.

[34] See Carrillo, R., "Violence against women: an obstacle to development", in Bunch, C. and Carrillo R., eds., *Gender Violence: A Development and Human Rights Issue* (New Jersey, Center for Women's Global Leadership, 1991).

[35] Moser, C. and Moser, A., "Background Paper on Gender-Based Violence", paper commissioned by the World Bank, Washington, D.C., 2003.

[36] See note 30; and http://www.un.org/womenwatch/daw/vaw/report.pdf; WHO, *Addressing violence against women and achieving the Millennium Development Goals* (Geneva, WHO, 2005).

[37] The lack of freedom from violence and physical security is identified as one of the critical indicators of inadequate governance, a critical constraint to the realization of the Millennium Development Goals. See Sachs, J., *Investing in Development: A Practical Plan to Achieve the Millennium Development Goals* (New York, Millennium Project, 2005).

[38] Platform for Action, para. 118.

[39] See Harway, M. and O'Neil, J., eds., *What causes men's violence against women* (Thousand Oaks, Sage Publications, 1999); *WHO Multi-Country Study on Women's Health and Domestic Violence Against Women: Initial Results on Prevalence, Health Outcomes and Women's Responses* (Geneva, WHO, 2005); and WHO, *World report on violence and health* (Geneva, WHO, 2002).

[40] See http://www.ohchr.org/english/about/publications/docs/FAQ_en.pdf; and Clapham, A., *Human Rights Obligations of Non-State Actors* (Oxford University Press, 2006).

[41] Michau, L. and Naker, D., eds., *Preventing gender-based violence in the Horn, East and Southern Africa: A regional dialogue* (Raising Voices and UN-Habitat Safer Cities Programme, 2004), pp. 7-8, available at: http://www.preventgbvafrica.org/images/publications/ reports/preventgbv_a.pdf.

[42] Mohanty, C.T., "Under western eyes: Feminist scholarship and colonial discourse", *Feminist Review*, vol. 30 (Autumn 1988), pp. 65-88.

[43] Chege, J., "Interventions linking gender relations and violence with reproductive health and HIV: rationale, effectiveness and gaps", *Gender, Culture and Rights, Agenda Special Focus*, vol. 115 (2005), pp. 114-123.

[44] Pelser, E., Gondwe, L., Mayamba, C., Mhango, T., Phiri, W. and Burton, P., *Intimate partner violence: Results from a national gender-based violence study in Malawi* (Pretoria, Institute for Security Studies, 2005), pp. 6-7, available at: http://www.issafrica.org/index.php?link_id=14&slink_id=185&link_type=12&slink_type=12&tmpl_id=3.

[45] World Health Organization, "Intimate partner violence and HIV/AIDS", WHO Information Bulletin Series, Number 1, available at http://www.who.int/gender/violence/en/ vawinformationbrief.pdf.

[46] Sideris, T., "Post-apartheid South Africa —Gender, rights and the politics of recognition—Continuities in gender-based violence?", *Gender, Culture and Rights, Agenda Special Focus*, vol. 115 (2005), pp. 100-109.

[47] *The State v. Baloyi*, Constitutional Court of South Africa, Case CCT 29/99, pp. 13-14 (footnotes omitted).

[48] Ibid, p. 13 (italics added).

[49] E/CN.4/2002/83.

[50] See Raday, F., "Culture, religion and gender", *I.CON*, vol. 1, No. 4 (2003), pp. 663-715.

[51] Mama, A., Melber, H. and Nyamnjoh, F. B., eds., "Concluding reflections on beyond identities: Rethinking power in Africa", *Identity and Beyond: Rethinking Africanity* (Uppsala, Nordic Africa Institute, 2001), p. 30.

[52] See E/CN.4/2003/75, paras. 61, 63; and Milillo, D., "Rape as a tactic of war: social and psychological perspectives" *Affilia*, vol. 21, No. 2, (2006), pp. 196-205.

[53] Jolly, S., *Gender and cultural change: Overview report* (Bridge, Institute of Development Studies, University of Sussex, 2002), p. 9.

[54] Potgieter, C., "Gender, culture and rights: challenges and approaches of three Chapter 9 Institutions", *Gender, Culture and Rights, Agenda Special Focus*, vol. 115 (2005), pp. 154-160, 159, quoting Chanock, M., "Culture and Human Rights: Orientalising, Occidentalising and Authenticity", in Mamdani, M., ed., *Beyond Rights Talk and Culture* (New York,
St. Martin's Press, 2000), p. 15.

[55] See note 1, para. 61; E/CN.4/2004/66; and E/CN.4/2002/83, para. 5.

[56] E/CN.4/2004/66, paras. 37, 38.

[57] E/CN.4/2003/75; Ibid.

[58] Alabama Coalition against Domestic Violence, information available at http://www.acadv.org/ dating.html.

[59] See note 53, p. 15.

[60] See Welchman, L. and Hossain, S., eds., *Honour—Crimes, paradigms, and violence against women* (London, Zed Books, 2005).

[61] See note 50.

[62] E/CN.4/2000/68/Add.5; and Merry, S. E., "Constructing a Global Law? Violence against Women and the Human Rights System", 28, Law and Social Inquiry (2003).

[63] See note 44, Organization of American States, "Trade liberalization, gender and development: What are the issues and how can we think about them?", paper prepared for the Second Ministerial Meeting on the Advancement of Women, Washington, D.C., 21-23 April 2004, available at http://www.oas.org/cim/REMIM%20II/CIM-REMIMII-doc.4ing.doc.

[64] See note 39, chap. 1.

[65] Sassen, S., "Women's Burden: Counter-Geographies of Globalization and the Feminization of Survival", *Nordic Journal of International Law*, vol. 71, No. 2 (2002), pp. 255-274.

[66] *2004 World Survey on the role of women in development: Women and international migration* (United Nations publication, Sales No. E.04.IV.4).

[67] E/CN.4/2006/61 (footnotes omitted).

[68] See Note 66.

[69] E/CN.4/1995/42.

[70] Human Rights Watch, *Gender-based violence against Kosovar Albanian women* (New York, Human Rights Watch, 2000), available at: http://www.hrw.org/reports/2000/fry/ Kosov003 02.htm#P113_16068.

[71] Thomas, D. and Beasley, M, "Domestic violence as a human rights issue", *Albany Law Review*, vol. 58 (1994-1995).

[72] See Heise, L., *Violence against women: An integrated, ecological framework* (New York, St. Martin's Press, 1998); note 39; Heise, L., Ellsberg, M. and Gottemoeller, M., "Ending violence against women", *Population Reports*, vol. 27, No. 11 (1999), pp. 8-38; and Jewkes, R., "Intimate Partner Violence: Causes and Prevention", *Lancet*, vol. 359 (2002), pp. 1423-1429.

[73] Jewkes, R., "Editorials: Preventing Domestic Violence", *British Medical Journal*, vol. 324 (2002), pp. 253-254 (italics added, footnote omitted), available at http://bmj.bmjjournals.com/ cgi/content/full/324/7332/253.

[74] See E/CN.4/2003/66/Add.1, para. 142.

[75] See note 49, recommendation 10.

[76] For description and evaluation of such programmes in several African countries, see note 41.

[77] See E/CN.4/2004/66, para. 69; and note 67, paras. 94-99.

[78] Watts, C. and Zimmerman, C., "Violence against women: global scope and magnitude", *Lancet*, vol. 359 (April 2002), pp. 1232-1237.

[79] Osattin, A., and Short, L., *Intimate partner violence and sexual assault: A guide to training materials and programs for health care providers* (Atlanta, Centers for Disease Control, National Center for Injury Prevention and Control, 1998).

[80] Saltzman, L., Fanslow, J. L., McMahon, P. M. and Shelley, G. A., *Intimate partner violence surveillance: Uniform definitions and recommended data elements, version 1.0.* (Atlanta, Centers for Disease Control and Prevention, National Center for Injury Prevention and Control, 2002).

[81] See note 39.

[82] Ibid.

[83] See note 72.

[84] The study covered 1,891 families. General Union of Women, Syrian Commission for Family Affairs, Violence against women study: Syria, supported by the United Nations Development Fund for Women, 2005.

[85] See note 39, p. 93.

[86] Coyne-Beasley, T., Moracco, K.E. and Casteel, M.J., "Adolescent femicide: a population-based study", *Archives of Pediatric and Adolescent Medicine*, vol. 157, No. 4 (April 2003), pp. 355-360.

[87] Paterson, K., *Femicide on the Rise in Latin America* (Silver City, International Relations Center, 2006).

[88] Gazmararian, J. A., Lazorick, S. et al., "Prevalence of violence against pregnant women", *Journal of the American Medical Association*, vol. 275, No. 24 (June 1996), pp. 1915-20.

[89] Almeras, D. et al., "Violence against women in couples: Latin America and the Caribbean. A proposal for measuring its incidence and trends", paper prepared for the International Meeting on Gender Statistics and Indicators for Measuring the Incidence of and Trends in Violence against Women in Latin America and the Caribbean, La Paz, 21-23 November 2001.

[90] Peedicayil, A., Sadowski, L. S., Jayaseelan, L., Shankar, V., Jain, D., Suresh, S. and Bangdiwala, S., "Spousal physical violence against women during pregnancy", *BJOG: An International Journal of Obstetrics and Gynecology*, vol. 111, No. 7 (July 2004), pp. 682-687; Nasir, K. and Hyder, A.A., "Violence against pregnant women in developing countries: review of evidence", *European Journal of Public Health*, vol. 13, No. 2 (June 2003), pp. 105-107. Campbell, J., Garcia-Moreno, C., and Sharps, P., "Abuse during pregnancy in industrialized and developing countries", *Violence against women*, vol. 10, No. 7 (July 2004), pp. 770-789.

[91] See note 39, p. 35.

[92] Ramiro, L., Hassan, F. and Peedicayil, A., "Risk markers of severe psychological violence against women: a WorldSAFE multi-country study", *Injury Control and Safety Promotion*, vol. 11, No. 2 (June 2004), pp. 131-137.

[93] Jaspard, M., Brown, E., Condon, S., Fougeyrollas-Schwebel, D., Houel, A., Lhomond, B. et al., *Les violences enver les femmes en France: Une enquête nationale* (Paris, CNRS, Universite de Paris Dauphine, 2001).

[94] Federal Ministry for Family Affairs, Senior Citizens, Women and Youth, *Health, well-being and personal safety of women in Germany: A representative study of violence against women in Germany* (Bonn, Federal Ministry for Family Affairs, Senior Citizens, Women and Youth, 2004). Central research results available at http://www.bmfsfj.de.

[95] See E/CN.4/Sub.2/2005/36.

[96] Other forms of traditional practices are identified in reports by States parties.

[97] UNICEF, *Female genital mutilation/Cutting: A statistical exploration* (New York, UNICEF, 2005); and UNICEF, *Changing a harmful social convention: female genital mutilation/cutting*, UNICEF Innocenti Digest (2005), available at http://www.unicef-icdc.org/publications/pdf/fgm-gb-2005.pdf.

[98] Ibid.

[99] Ibid.

[100] Krantz, G. and Garcia-Moreno, C., "Violence against women", *Journal of Epidemiology and Community Health*, vol. 58 (2005), pp. 818-821.

[101] Prabhat, J. et al., "Low male to female sex ratio of children born in India: national survey of 1.1 million households", *Lancet*, vol. 367 (January 2006), pp. 211-18.

[102] Hong, M.S., "Boy preference and imbalance in sex ratio in Korea", paper prepared for the UNFPA/KIHASA International Symposium on Issues Related to Sex Preference for Children in the Rapidly Changing Demographic Dynamics in Asia, Seoul, 21-24 November 1994.

[103] While the definition in the Convention on the Rights of the Child states that "a child is a person below the age of 18 years unless under the law applicable to the child, majority is obtained earlier", the Committee on the Elimination of Discrimination against Women considers that the minimum age for marriage should be 18 years for both man and woman and that marriage should not be permitted before they have attained full maturity and capacity to act. See general recommendation No. 21 (1994). See note 24.

[104] Committee on the Elimination of Discrimination against Women general recommendation No. 21, referring to WHO. See note 24.

[105] UNAIDS/UNFPA/UNIFEM, *Women and HIV: Confronting the Crisis*, 2004.

[106] See Mathur, S., Greene, M. and Malhotra, A., *Too young to wed: The lives, rights, and health of young married girls* (Washington, D.C.: International Center for Research on Women, 2003).

[107] Population Council, Briefing sheet, *Child Marriage Briefing—Ethiopia* (July 2004), available at http://www.popcouncil.org/pdfs/briefingsheets/Ethiopia.pdf.

[108] See note 39; Vlachova, M. and Biason, L., 2005, *Women in an Insecure World: Violence against Women, Facts, Figures, and Analysis* (Geneva, Geneva Centre for the Democratic Control of Armed Forces, 2005).

[109] UNICEF, *Early marriage: A harmful traditional practice: A statistical exploration* (New York, UNICEF, 2005); Estimates are given in World Marriage Patterns (United Nations publication, Sales No. E.00.XIII.7).

[110] Article 16 (1) (b) of the Convention on the Elimination of All Forms of Discrimination against Women requires that States parties ensure to women "the same right freely to choose a spouse and to enter into marriage only with their free and full consent". See also art. 23(3) of the International Covenant on Civil and Political Rights.

[111] Rude-Antoine, E., *Forced marriages in Council of Europe member states* (Strasbourg, Directorate General of Human Rights, Council of Europe, 2005).

[112] Kleinbach, R., "Frequency of Non-Consensual Bride Kidnapping in the Kyrgyz Republic", *International Journal of Central Asian Studies*, vol. 8, No. 1 (2003).

[113] Home Office, *Dealing with Cases of Forced Marriage: Guidance for Education Professionals* (London, Foreign and Commonwealth Office, 2005).

[114] Indian Ministry of Home Affairs Parliamentary Questionnaire, 16 August 2004, cited in: Immigration and Nationality Directorate, Report of the Fact-Finding Mission to India: Women in India, 11-24 July 2004 (London, United Kingdom Home Office, 2004).

[115] See Mohanty, M. K., Panigrahi, M. K., Mohanty, S. and Das, S. K., "Victimologic study of female homicide", *Legal Issues in Medicine*, vol. 6, No. 3 (July 2004), pp. 151-156.

[116] UNFPA, *State of World Population 2000* (New York, UNFPA, 2000); Kogacioglu, D., 2004. "The tradition effect: Framing honor crimes in Turkey", *Differences: A Journal of Feminist Cultural Studies*, vol. 15, No. 2 (2004), pp. 119-151.

[117] Combined initial, second and third periodic reports of Pakistan submitted under article 18 of the Convention on the Elimination of all Forms of Discrimination against Women, para. 529, CEDAW/C/PAK/1-3.

[118] Adinkrah, M., "Witchcraft accusation and female homicide victimization in contemporary Ghana", *Violence against women*, vol. 10, No. 4 (December 2004), pp. 325-356.

[119] Saravanan, S., *Violence against women in India: A literature review* (New Delhi, Institute of Social Studies Trust, 2000); Chen, M. A., "Widowhood and aging in India", United Nations Research Institute for Social Development case study available at: http://www.unrisd.org/unrisd/website/projects.nsf/(httpAuxPages)/25DCC0F9F3E206C3C1256BB200552FC6?OpenDocument&category=Case+Studies.

[120] CEDAW/C/2005/OP.8/Mexico.

[121] E/CN.4/2005/72/Add.3.

[122] Consideration of the sixth periodic report of Guatemala submitted under article 18 of the Convention on the Elimination of All Forms of Discrimination against Women, Department of Public Information of the United Nations, 18 May 2006, available at: http://www.un.org/NEWS/Press/docs/2006/wom1559.doc.htm.

[123] See report of the Inter American Commission on Human Rights Special Rapporteur on the rights of women, The Situation of the Rights of Women in Ciudad Juárez, Mexico: The Right to be Free from Violence and Discrimination, March 2003; E/CN.4/2005/72/Add.3; and note 87.

[124] See note 39.

[125] Health Canada, *Women's health surveillance report: A multi-dimensional look at the health of Canadian women* (Ontario, Canadian Institute for Health Information, 2003); Tjaden, P. and Thoennes, N., Prevalence, *Incidence and Consequences of Violence Against Women: Findings from the National Violence Against Women Study*, Research in Brief series No. 2 (Washington D.C., National Institute of Justice and Centers for Disease Control, 1998), available at http://www.ncjrs.gov/pdffiles/172837.pdf.

[126] See note 39.

[127] Violence experienced by women in Switzerland over their lifetime: Results of the International Violence against Women Survey (IVAWS), 2006.

[128] See note 39.

[129] Byers, S., Sears, H., Whelan, J. and Saint-Pierre, M., *Dating Violence Amongst New Brunswick Adolescents: A Summary of Two Studies*, Research Paper Series No. 2 (Fredericton, University of New Brunswick, Muriel McQueen Fergusson Centre for Family Violence Research, 2000).

[130] Centers for Disease Control and Prevention (2000), *Dating violence*, National Center for Injury Prevention and Control.

[131] Slashinski, M., Coker, L. A. and Davis, E. K., "Physical aggression, forced sex, and stalking victimization by a dating partner: an analysis of the national violence against women survey", *Violence and Victims*, vol. 18, No. 6 (December 2003), pp. 595-617.

[132] E/CN.4/2005/72, paras. 37 and 38.

[133] Directorate-General for Employment, Industrial Relations and Social Affairs, *Sexual harassment at the workplace in the European Union* (European Commission, 1998).

[134] See ILO, "Action against sexual harassment at work in Asia and the Pacific", technical report for discussion at the ILO/Japan regional tripartite seminar on action against sexual harassment at work in Asia and the Pacific, Penang, Malaysia, 2-4 October 2001.

[135] American Association of University Women, *Hostile Hallways: bullying, teasing, and sexual harassment in school* (Washington D.C., American Association of University Women, 2001).

[136] Cited in Wellesley Centers for Research on Women, Unsafe Schools: A Literature Review of School-Related Gender-Based Violence in Developing Countries (Arlington, Development and Training Services, Inc., 2004).

[137] Action Aid and UNICEF commissioned survey on gender violence in Malawi cited in IRIN News report, "Malawi: Abuse of women a national shame", United Nations Office for the Coordination of Humanitarian Affairs, available at: http://www.irinnews.org/report.asp?ReportID=51488&SelectRegion=Southern_Africa& SelectCountry=MALAWI

[138] Bradley, R. C., *Abuso en el deporte* (Mexico City, Mexico, D.F., 2006), p. 3.

[139] Fasting, K. and Knorre, N., *Women in Sport in the Czech Republic: The Experiences of Female Athletes*. Norwegian School of Sports Sciences and Czech Olympic Committee (Oslo and Praha 2005), pp. 42-43.

[140] General Assembly resolution 55/25, article 3 (a).

[141] All data taken from: *Trafficking in persons. Global patterns*, United Nations Office on Drugs and Crime, Vienna, April 2006.

[142] Ibid.

[143] E/CN.4/1992/SR.21, para. 35.

[144] See E/CN.4/1998/54; E/CN.4/2004/66/Add.1; Human Rights Watch, *All too familiar: Sexual abuse of women in U.S. state prisons* (1996); Arbour, L. Commission of Inquiry into certain events at the Prison for women in Kingston (Public Works and Government Services, Canada, 1996).

[145] See Taylor, R., *Women in prison and children of imprisoned mothers, Preliminary research report* (New York, Quaker United Nations Office, 2004).

[146] Final report by the Commissioner For Human Rights, *On The Human.Rights Situation Of The Roma, Sinti And Travellers In Europe*, for the attention of the Committee of Ministers and the Parliamentary Assembly, paras. 71-74.

[147] Amnesty International, *Stolen Sisters: Discrimination and Violence Against Indigenous Women in Canada. A Summary of Amnesty International's Concerns* (London, Amnesty International, 2004).

[148] NGO Working Group on Women, Peace and Security, Fact Sheet on Women and Armed Conflict, October 23, 2002, available at: http://www.iwtc.org/212.html.

[149] Ibid.

[150] Ibid.

[151] In humanitarian settings, attention is commonly placed on gender-based violence (of which sexual violence is a form). Although sexual violence is perpetrated primarily by men against women, men and boys may also be subject to gender-based violence.

[152] See note 148.

[153] Ibid.

[154] Crenshaw, K. "Mapping the margins: Intersectionality, identity politics and violence against women of color", *Stanford Law Review*, vol. 43, No. 6 (1991), pp. 1241-1299.

[155] See note 149.

[156] Ibid.

[157] Ibid.

[158] Bhandari, N., "Aboriginal violence against women", *Contemporary Review* (December 2003).

[159] Grey, M., "Dalit women and the struggle for justice", *Feminist Theology*, vol. 14, No. 1 (2005), pp. 127-149.

[160] Amnesty International, "Violence against women: A fact sheet", available at: http://www.amnestyusa.org/stopviolence/factsheets/violence.html.

[161] See note 3.

[162] Human Rights Watch, "Women and girls with disabilities", available at: http://hrw.org/women/disabled.html.

[163] See note 66, p. 1.

[164] E/CN.4/2000/76, para. 8

[165] E/CN.4/2000/76, para. 12; Esim, S. and Smith, M., "Gender and Migration in Arab States: the Case of Domestic Workers" (Beirut, International Labour Organization Regional Office for Arab States, 2004).

[166] See note 66.

[167] Office of the United Nations High Commissioner for Refugees, 2005 Global Refugee Trends, http://www.unhcr.org/cgi-bin/texis/vtx/events/opendoc.pdf?tbl=STA-TISTICS&id=4486ceb12.

[168] Heise, L., "Violence against women: The hidden health burden", *World Health Statistics Quarterly*, vol. 46, No. 1 (1993), pp. 78-85.

[169] Laffaye, C., Kennedy, C. and Stein, M. B., "Post-traumatic stress disorder and health-related quality of life in female victims of intimate partner violence", *Violence Victims*, vol. 18, No. 2 (April 2003), pp. 227-238; Paranjape, A., Heron, S. and Kaslow, N., 2005. "Utilization of Services by Abused, Low-Income African-American Women", *Journal of General Internal Medicine*, vol. 21, No. 2 (February 2006), p. 22.

[170] Cohen, M. M. and Maclean, H., "Violence against Canadian Women", *BMC Womens Health*, vol. 4, (Suppl. 1) (August 2004), pp. S22-S46; Silverman, J., Raj, A., Mucci, L. and Hathaway, J., "Dating violence against adolescent girls and associated substance use, unhealthy weight control, sexual risk behavior, pregnancy, and suicidality", *Journal of the American Medical Association*, vol. 286, No. 5 (August 2001), pp. 372-379.

[171] Ganatra, B., Coyaji, K. and Rao, V., "Too far, too little, too late: a community-based case-control study of maternal mortality in rural west Maharashtra, India", *Bulletin of the World Health Organization*, vol. 76, No. 6 (1998), pp. 591-598.

[172] Fauveau, V. et al., "Causes of maternal mortality in rural Bangladesh, 1976-85", *Bulletin of the World Health Organization*, vol. 66, No. 5 (March-April 1988), pp. 643-651; see note 39.

[173] Heise, L., Ellsberg, M. and Gottemoeller M., "A global overview of gender-based violence", *International Journal of Gynaecology and Obstetrics*, vol. 78, Suppl. 1 (2002), pp. S3-S14; UNICEF, "Domestic violence against women and girls", *Innocenti Digest*, No. 6 (June 2000).

[174] Campbell, J. C., "Health consequences of intimate partner violence", *Lancet*, vol. 359, No. 9314 (April 2002), pp. 1331-1336.

[175] Global Coalition on Women and AIDS, background paper on "Violence against women and AIDS" available at http://data.unaids.org/GCWA/GCWA_BG_Violence_en.pdf; amfAR, *Gender-based violence and HIV among women: Assessing the evidence*, Issue Brief No. 3, June 2005; and Human Rights Watch, *Just die quietly: Domestic violence and women's vulnerability to HIV in Uganda*, August 2003.

[176] See note 108.

[177] Pallitto, C., "Relationship between intimate partner violence and unintended pregnancy: Analysis of a national sample from Colombia", *International Family Planning Perspectives*, vol. 30, No. 4 (December 2004), pp. 165-173.

[178] Leung W. C. et al., "Pregnancy outcome following domestic violence in a Chinese community", *International Journal of Gynaecology and Obstetrics*, vol. 71, No. 1 (January 2001), pp. 79-80; and Valladares E. M. et al., "Physical partner abuse during pregnancy: a risk factor for low birth weight in Nicaragua", *Obstetrics & Gynecology*, vol. 100, No. 4 (October 2002), pp. 700-705.

[179] Ibid.

[180] Palmerlee, A., *Human trafficking: combating an international crisis* (St. Leonards, N.S.W., Centre for Independent Studies, 2004), p. 4.

[181] See note 97, chapter 4.

[182] See note 174.

[183] Tolman, R. and Rosen, D., "Domestic violence in the lives of women receiving welfare: Mental health, substance dependences and economic well-being", *Violence against women*, vol. 7 (February 2001), pp. 141-158.

[184] See note 39; Haarr, R., *Violence against women in marriage: A general population study in Khatlon Oblast, Tajikistan* (Dushanbe, Project to Reduce Violence against Women—PROVAW, Social Development Group, 2005).

[185] Mulugeta, E., Kassaye, M. and Berhane, Y., "Prevalence and outcomes of sexual violence among high school students", *Ethiopian Medical Journal*, vol. 36, No. 3 (July 1998), pp. 167-174; Bagley, C., Bolitho, F. and Bertrand, L., "Sexual assault in school, mental health and suicidal behaviors in adolescent women in Canada", *Adolescence*, vol. 32, No. 126 (Summer 1997), pp. 361-366.

[186] See note 72.

[187] Lyon, E., "Welfare and Domestic Violence Against Women: Lessons from Research", *Applied Research Forum, National Electronic Network on Violence Against Women* (August 2002), available at http://www.vawnet.org/DomesticViolence/Research/VAWnetDocs/AR_Welfare2.pdf.; Morrison, A. and Biehl, L., eds., *Too Close to Home: Domestic Violence in the Americas* (Washington D.C., Inter-American Development Bank, 1999).

[188] Goetz, A. M., "Conditions for Women's Political Effectiveness: A Conceptual Framework", paper presented at the conference on EnGendering Processes of Governance at Global, Regional and National Levels, University of Warwick, 19 September 2002; Center for Women's Global Leadership and International Gay and Lesbian Human Rights Commission, *Written Out: How Sexuality is Used to Attack Women's Organizing* (Rutgers, Center for Women's Global Leadership, International Gay and Lesbian Human Rights Commission, 2005); for specific incidents of violence against women activists and leaders see: http://www.cwru.edu/provost/centerforwomen/writtenout.pdf.

[189] Mumtaz, K., "Women's Representation, Effectiveness and Leadership in South Asia", background paper prepared for the Fifth South Asia Regional Ministerial Conference, Islamabad, Pakistan, 3-5 May 2005.

[190] See note 72.

[191] See note 180.

[192] Moser, C. and Clark, F. C., eds., *Victims, Perpetrators or Actors? Gender, Armed Conflict and Political Violence* (London, Zed Books, 2001).

[193] Osofsky, J., "The Impact of Violence on Children", *The future of children: Domestic violence and children*, vol. 9, No. 3 (Winter 1999), pp. 33-49; Margolin, G. and Gordis E. B., "The effects of family and community violence on children", *Annual Review of Psychology*, vol. 51 (February 2000), pp. 445-479.

[194] See note 187, Morrison, A. and Orlando, M. B., "Social and economic costs of domestic violence: Chile and Nicaragua".

[195] Kitzmann, K. M. et al., "Child witnesses to domestic violence: A meta-analytic review", *Journal of Consulting and Clinical Psychology*, vol. 71, No. 2 (April 2003), pp. 339-352.

[196] See note 193.

[197] Edleson, J., "Problems associated with children's witnessing of domestic violence", *Applied Research Forum National Electronic Forum on Violence against Women* (April 1999), available at:
http://www.vawnet.org/DomesticViolence/Research/VAWnetDocs/AR_witness.pdf.

[198] Larraín, S., Vega, J. and Delgado, I., *Relacionares Familiares y Maltrato Infantil* (Santiago, UNICEF, 1997).

[199] Merrill, L., Thomsen, C., Crouch, J., May, P., Gold, S. and Milner, J., "Predicting risk of child physical abuse from childhood exposure to violence: Can interpersonal schemata explain the association?", *Journal of Social and Clinical Psychology*, vol. 24, No. 7 (December 2005), pp. 981-1002.

[200] Asling-Monemi, K. et al., "Violence against women increases the risk of infant and child mortality: a case-referent study from Nicaragua", *Bulletin of the World Health Organization*, vol. 81, No. 1 (2003), pp. 10-16.

[201] Council of Europe, *Combating violence against women: Stocktaking study on the measures and actions taken in the Council of Europe member states*, 2006, p. 8.

[202] Heise, L., Pitanguy, J. and Germain, A., *Violence against Women: The Hidden Health Burden*, World Bank Discussion Paper 255 (Washington D.C., World Bank, 1994).

[203] Greaves, L., Hakivsky, O. et al., *Selected Estimates of the costs of Violence Against Women* (London, Centre of Research on Violence against Women and Children, 1995).

[204] Walby, S., *The cost of domestic violence* (London, Department of Trade and Industry, 2004), available at:
http://www.womenandequalityunit.gov.uk/research/cost_of_dv_Report_sept04.pdf.

[205] Heiskanen, M. and Piispa, M., *The price of violence: The costs of men's violence against women in Finland* (Helsinki, Statistics Finland, Ministry of Social Affairs and Health, 2001).

[206] World Bank, *World Development Report 1993: Investing in health* (New York, Oxford University Press, 1993).

[207] *The World's Women 2005: Progress in statistics* (United Nations publication, Sales No. E.05.XVII.7).

[208] See Division for the Advancement of Women, "Violence against women: a statistical overview, challenges and gaps in data collection and methodology and approaches for overcoming them", report of the expert group meeting organized in collaboration with the Economic Commission for Europe and World Health Organization, Geneva, 11-14 April 2005, available at http://www.un.org/womenwatch/daw/egm/vaw-stat-2005/index.html.

[209] Australian Bureau of Statistics, *Women's Safety Australia*, Catalogue 4128.0 (Canberra, Australian Bureau of Statistics, 1996).

[210] Heiskanen, M. and Piispa, M., Faith, Hope, *Battering. A survey of men's violence against women in Finland* (Helsinki, Statistics Finland and Council for Equality, Ministry of Social Affairs and Health, 1998).

[211] See note 93.

[212] See note 94.

[213] Morris, A., *Women's safety survey 1996* (Wellington, Institute of Criminology, University of Wellington, 1997).

[214] Lundgren, E., Heimer, G., Westerstand, J. and Kalliokoski, A-M., *Captured queen: Men's violence against women in "equal" Sweden: A prevalence study* (Umeå, Fritzes Offentliga Publikationer; 2001).

[215] Tjaden, P. and Thoennes, N., Extent, *Nature and Consequences of Intimate Partner Violence: Findings from the National Violence against Women Survey* (Washington, D.C., National Institute of Justice, Centers for Disease Control and Prevention, 2000).

[216] Coordinated by the European Institute for Crime Prevention and Control, with inputs from the United Nations Office on Drugs and Crime, Statistics Canada and the United Nations Interregional Crime and Justice Research Institute.

[217] ECE/CES/2006/7, paras 28-29.

[218] Kishor, S. and Johnson, K., *Domestic violence in nine developing countries: A comparative study* (Calverton, Macro International, 2004).

[219] Yoder, S., Abderrahim N. and Zhuahuni A., *Female genital cutting in the Demographic and Health Surveys: A critical and comparative analysis* (Calverton, Macro International, 2004); see note 112.

[220] Velzeboer, M., Ellsberg, M., Clavel, C. and Garcia-Moreno C., *Violence against women: The health sector responds*, Occasional publication No. 12 (Washington, D.C., Pan American Health Organization, 2003).

[221] Sagot, M., "The critical path of women affected by family violence in Latin America: Case studies from 10 countries", *Violence against women*, vol. 11, No. 10 (October 2005), pp. 1292-1318.

[222] Igras, S., Monahan, B. and Syphrines, O., *Issues and Responses to Sexual Violence: Assessment Report of the Dadaab Refugee Camps, Kenya* (Nairobi, CARE International, 1998).

[223] Bott, S., Morrison, A. and Ellsberg, M., *Preventing and responding to gender-based violence in middle and low-income countries: A global review and analysis* (Washington, D.C., World Bank, 2004).

[224] See note 123; E/CN.4/2005/72/Add.3; Amnesty International, *Mexico: Ending the brutal cycle of violence against women in Ciudad Juárez and the city of Chihuahua* (London, Amnesty International, 2004); Amnesty International, *Guatemala: No protection, no justice: Killings of women in Guatemala* (London, Amnesty International, 2005), available at: http://web.amnesty.org/library/Index/ENGAMR340172005; see note 87.

[225] Frye, V., Hosein, V., Waltermaurer, E., Blaney, S. and Wilt, S., "The epidemiology of femicide in New York City: 1990-1999", *Homicide Studies*, vol. 9, No. 3 (2005), pp. 204-228; Sharma B., Harish D., Gupta, M. and Singh, V., "Dowry: A deep-rooted cause of violence against women in India", *Medicine, Science and the Law*, vol. 45, No. 2 (April 2005), pp. 45:161-168; Pratt, C. and Deosaransingh, K., "Gender differences in homicide in Contra Costa County, California: 1982-1993", *American Journal of Preventive Medicine*, vol. 13, No. 6 (November-December 1997), pp. 19-24; Parsons, L. H. and Harper, M. A., "Violent maternal deaths in North Carolina", *Obstetrics and Gynecology*, vol. 94, No. 6 (December 1999), pp. 990-993.

[226] Ibid., Sharma, B., note; Hadidi, M., Kulwicki, A. and Jahshan, H., "A review of 16 cases of honour killings in Jordan in 1995", *International Journal of Legal Medicine*, vol. 114, No. 6 (July 2001), pp. 357-359; Kardam, F., Alpar, Z., Yuksel, I. and Ergun, E., *The Dynamics of Honor Killings in Turkey: Prospects for Action* (Ankara, UNDP/UNFPA, 2005); Kumar, V., "Poisoning deaths in married women", *Journal of Clinical Forensic Medicine*, vol. 11, No. 1 (February 2004), pp. 2-5; Mago, V., Ahmad, I., Kochhar, N. and Bariar, L. M., "Burnt pregnant wives: a social stigma", *Burns*, vol. 31, No. 2 (March 2005), pp. 175-177; Mohanty, M. K., Arun, M, Monteiro, F.N. and Palimar, V., "Self-inflicted burns fatalities in Manipal, India", *Medicine, Science and the Law*, vol. 45, No. 1 (January 2005), pp. 27-30; Kulwicki, A. D., "The practice of honor crimes: a glimpse of domestic violence in the Arab world", *Issues in Mental Health Nursing*, vol. 23, No. 1 (January-February 2002), pp. 77-87.

[227] Campbell, J. C., Webster, D., Koziol-McLain, J., Block, C., Campbell, D. and Curry, M.A. et al., "Risk factors for femicide in abusive relationships: results from a multisite case control study", *American Journal of Public Health*, vol. 93, No. 7 (July 2003), pp. 1089-1097.

[228] Ibid.

[229] Amowitz, L., Reis, C., Lyons, K., Vann, B., Mandalay, G., Akinsulure-Smith, A. et al., "Prevalence of war-related sexual violence and other human rights abuses among internally displaced persons in Sierra Leone", *Journal of the American Medical Association*, vol. 287, No. 4 (January 2002), pp. 513-521; Swiss, S., Jennings, P. J., Aryee, G. V. et al. "Violence against women during the Liberian civil conflict", *Journal of the American Medical Association*, vol. 279, No. 8 (February 1998), pp. 625-629; Ward, J. and Vann, B., "Gender-based violence in refugee settings", *Lancet*, vol. 360, Suppl. (December 2002), pp. 13-14; Hynes, M., Ward, J., Robertson, K. and Crouse, C., "A determination of the prevalence of gender-based violence among conflict-affected populations in East Timor", *Disasters*, vol. 28, No. 3 (September 2004), pp. 294-321; and Giller, J., Bracken, P. and Kabaganda, S., "Uganda: War, Women and Rape", *Lancet*, vol. 337, No. 604 (March 1991).

[230] Developed with the Centers for Disease Control and the University of Arizona. See note 229; Reproductive Health Response in Conflict Consortium, *Gender-based Violence Tools Manual for Assessment and Program Design, Monitoring, and Evaluation in Conflict-affected Settings* (New York, Reproductive Health Response in Conflict Consortium, 2004).

[231] This section is based on Aronowitz, A., *Data on Trafficking in Women*, New York: United Nations Division for the Advancement of Women, 2005.

[232] Kelly, E. and Regan, L., *Stopping traffic: Exploring the extent of, and responses to trafficking in women for sexual exploitation in the UK* (London, Policing and Reducing Crime Unit, Research, Development and Statistics Directorate, Home Office, 2000).

[233] Makkai, T., "Thematic discussion on trafficking in human beings", paper prepared for the Workshop on trafficking in human beings, especially women and children, held as part of the twelfth session of the Commission on Crime Prevention and Criminal Justice, Vienna, 15 May 2003.

[234] For example, global and regional data collection efforts are being carried out by the International Organization for Migration Counter Trafficking Module Database, the Innocenti Research Centre of UNICEF, The Global Programme against Trafficking in Human Beings Database of the United Nations Office on Drugs and Crime, the OSCE-Regional Clearing Point of the Stability Pact Task Force on Trafficking in the Balkans and the Protection Project of Johns Hopkins School of Advanced International Studies.

[235] See note 136; Leach, F., Fiscian, V., Kadzamira, E., Lemani E. and Machakanja, P., *An Investigative Study of the Abuse of Girls in African Schools* (London, Department for International Development, 2003).

[236] d'Oliveira, A. F., Diniz, S. G. and Schraiber, L. B., "Violence against women in health-care institutions: an emerging problem", *Lancet*, vol. 359, No. 9318 (May 2002), pp. 1681-1685.

[237] See note 30; Walby, S., *Developing indicators on violence against women*. New York: United Nations Division for the Advancement of Women, 2005; Almeras, D., Bravo, R., Milsavljevic, V., Montaño, D. and Rico, M. N., *Violence against women in couples: Latin America and the Caribbean. A proposal for measuring its incidence and trends* (Santiago, Economic Commission for Latin America and the Caribbean, 2004). The United Nations Economic Commission for Africa has developed an African Gender and Development Index, consisting of the Gender Status Index and the African Women's Progress Scoreboard. The Gender Status Index is quantitative, whereas the African Women's Progress Scoreboard captures qualitative issues in relation to the performance of gender policies of African Governments, including indicators on violence against women. See http://www.uneca.org/eca_programmes/acgd/Publications/AGDI_book_final.pdf.

[238] Commission on Human Rights resolution 2004/46.

[239] See note 30.

[240] Dijkstra, A.G., "Revisiting UNDP's GDI and GEM: Towards an Alternative", *Social Indicators Research*, vol. 57, No. 3 (March 2002), pp. 301-338; Hirway, I. and Mahadevia, D., "Critique of Gender Development Index: Towards an Alternative", *Economic and Political Weekly*, vol. 31, No. 43 (October 1996), pp. 87-96; Bardhan, K. and Klasen, S., "UNDP's Gender-Related indices: A Critical Review", *World Development*, vol. 27, No. 6 (June 1999), pp. 985-1010.

[241] See note 208.

[242] These rights are set out in the Universal Declaration of Human Rights, articles 3, 4, 5, 7, 16 and 25; and guaranteed by treaties including the International Covenant on Civil and Political Rights, articles 6, 7, 8, 9, 23, 26 and the International Covenant on Economic, Social and Cultural Rights, articles 7, 11 and 12. See also Committee on the Elimination of Discrimination against Women general recommendation 19, para 7. See note 24.

Ending violence against women: From words to action

[243] *Women, Peace and Security* (United Nations publication, Sales No. E.03.IV.1), p. 33.

[244] Committee on the Elimination of Discrimination against Women general recommendation No. 12. See note 24.

[245] *Carmichele v. Minister of Safety and Security* 2001 (10) BCLR 995 (CC) at para. 62.

[246] See Cook, R., ed., *The Human Rights of Women: National and International Perspectives* (Philadelphia, University of Pennsylvania Press, 1994); Cook, R., ed., "State Responsibility for Violations of Women's Human Rights", *Harvard Human Rights Journal*, vol. 125 (1994), p. 137.

[247] This terminology was first elaborated by the Special Rapporteur of the Sub-commission on the right to adequate food as a human right (E/CN.4/Sub.2/1987/23 paras. 66-69), and has subsequently been advanced by Committee on Economic, Social and Cultural Rights general comment No. 14 (HRI/GEN/1/Rev.8); On the general issue of responsibility of States for internationally wrongful acts, see the articles on responsibility of States for internationally wrongful acts, adopted by the International Law Commission at its 53rd session, annexed to General Assembly resolution 56/83.

[248] See HRI/GEN/1/Rev.8, 8 May 2006, para. 27.

[249] See General Assembly resolution 56/83, article 5. It has been argued that this definition includes public corporations, quasi-public entities and certain private companies. See Crawford, J., *The International Law Commission's Articles on State Responsibility: Introduction, Text and Commentary* (Cambridge, University of Cambridge, 2002), p. 10. See also article 8.

[250] See Convention on the Elimination of All Forms of Discrimination against Women, article 2 (e); Chirwa, D., "The doctrine of state responsibility as a potential means of holding private actors accountable for human rights", *Melbourne Law Journal*, vol. 5 (2004), p. 5.

[251] See Committee on the Elimination of Discrimination against Women general recommendation 19, article 24 (i); note 15, article 4 (d).

[252] See Committee on the Elimination of Discrimination against Women general recommendation 19, para. 24 (a); note 15, para. 4 (c); note 22, para. 124 (b); note 23, para. 13; Inter-American Convention on the Prevention, Punishment and Eradication of Violence against women (Convention of Belém do Pará), article 7 (b).

[253] *Velasquez Rodriguez v. Honduras*, Judgment of July 29, 1988, Inter-American Court of Human Rights (Ser. C) No. 4, 1988.

[254] Ibid. para. 175; *Osman v. United Kingdom*—(28 October 1998) [Grand Chamber] (2000) 29 EHRR 245.

[255] See E/CN.4/1997/47 and E/CN.4/2006/61 paras. 35 and 36.

[256] See note 254; *E. and Others v. The United Kingdom*—33218/96 [2002] ECHR 769.

[257] A/51/44.

[258] *Algür v. Turkey*, European Court of Human Rights, 32574/96 (22 October 2002).

[259] *Ana, Beatriz and Celia Gonzales Perez v. Mexico*, Inter-American Commission on Human Rights Case 11.565, No. 53/01, 4 April 2001.

[260] See *The Prosecutor v. Jean-Paul Akayesu*, Case No. ICTR-96-4-T, 2 September 1998; *Prosecutor v. Dragoljub Kunarac, Radomir Kovac, and Zoran Vukovic*—Appeals Chamber—Judgment—IT-96-23 &23 /1 [2002] ICTY 2 (12 June 2002).

[261] *The Prosecutor v. Jean-Paul Akayesu*, Case. No. ICTR-96-4-T, 2 September 1998.

[262] Forced marriage has been charged as an "inhumane act" under article 2 (i) of the Statute. See also: Special Court for Sierra Leone: Decision on Prosecution Request for Leave to Amend the Indictment, SCSL-04-16 (AFRC), 6 May 2004.

[263] Rome Statute of the International Criminal Court, article 7, para 1. See also article 8, paras. 1 and 2 (b) on war crimes.

[264] See note 9, paras. 124 (e) and (f); Declaration on the Elimination of Violence against Women, article 4 (a); note 23, para. 68 (c) and (d).

[265] Convention on the Elimination of All Forms of Discrimination against Women, article 2; note 19, para. 232 (b); see Committee on the Elimination of Discrimination against Women general recommendation 19, paras. 1, 4, 6, 7.

[266] See note 15, article 4 (e); note 19, para. 124 (p); note 20, para. 76.

[267] See note 15, article 4 (h); note 19, para. 124 (p).

[268] See note 19, paras. 124 (c), 124 (d), 124 (i) and 124 (o), along with 283 (a) and 283 (d) in relation to the girl child; note 20, paras. 69 (a), 69 (d), 69 (e); note 15, article 4 (d); Committee on the Elimination of Discrimination against Women general recommendation 19, para. 24 (b); note 252, Belém do Pará, article 7 (c) and (e); *A.T. v. Hungary*, communication No. 2/2003; views adopted 26 January 2005, at 9.6.II v; and *MC v. Bulgaria*, European Court of Human Rights 39272/98, 4 December 2003.

[269] Ibid., *A.T. v. Hungary*.

[270] *X and Y v. the Netherlands*, European Court of Human Rights 8978/80, 1985; note 247, p. 144.

[271] *Maria Mamerita Mestanza Chavez v. Peru*, Inter-American Commission of Human Rights, Case 12.191, No. 66/00, 2000.

[272] See note 268, para. 174.

[273] See note 19, paras. 124 (b), 143 (c), 145 (d) and (e) and 147 (c); note 20, para. 13; note 15, article 4 (c); note 253, Belém do Pará, article 7 (b).

[274] General Assembly resolution 52/86; A/52/635, para 8 (b).

[275] See note 268, *A.T. v. Hungary*, at 9.6 II (vi).

[276] See note 268, *MC v. Bulgaria*.

[277] Ibid., paras. 177 and 185.

[278] Ibid., para. 8 (c).

[279] See note 15, articles 4 (c) and (d); note 277, Belém do Pará, article 7 (b) and (c); note 19, paras. 124 (c), 124 (o) and 130 (b).

[280] *Maria da Penha Maia Fernandes v. Brazil*, Inter-American Commission on Human Rights, Case 12.051, 16 April 2002.

[281] Ibid., para. 55.

[282] See note 120, paras. 273 and 274.

[283] See note 19, para. 124 (g).

[284] Committee on the Elimination of Discrimination against Women general recommendation 19, para. 24 (i); note 15, article 4 (d); note 23, para. 69 (b); Rome Statute, article 79; note 277, Belém do Pará, article 7 (g); note 299, annex, para. 10 (c); E/CN.4/2000/62, 2000, annex, preamble.

[285] See note 268, *A.T. v. Hungary*, para. 9.6 I (ii).

[286] See note 280, recommendation 3 and para. 61.

[287] See note 19, para. 125 (a) and (j) and, in relation to the girl child, para. 283 (d); Committee on the Elimination of Discrimination against Women general recommendation 19, para. 24 (b); note 252, Belém do Pará, article 8 (d); E/CN.4/2006/61, para 74; note 268, *A.T. v. Hungary*.

[288] See note 268, *A.T. v. Hungary*, at 9.3.

[289] Convention on the Elimination of All Forms of Discrimination against Women, article 2 (f) and 5 (a).

[290] See note 252, Belém do Pará, article 7 (e).

[291] Protocol to the African Charter on the Rights of Women in Africa, articles 2 (2) and 5.

[292] Convention on the Elimination of All Forms of Discrimination against Women, article 5 (a); note 252, Belém do Pará, article 8 (b); Protocol to the African Charter on the Rights of Women in Africa, article 4 (d).

[293] See note 19, para. 124 (a); note 15, article 4; note 268, *A.T. v. Hungary*; Human Rights Committee general comment No. 28 (2002), para. 5.

[294] See note 120, para 287.

[295] See note 268, *A.T. v. Hungary*.

[296] See note 15, article 4 (h); note 19, paras. 124 (g), 124 (n); note 23, para. 78 (d); note 20, pp. 276, 278, 286 and 288; note 268, *A.T. v. Hungary*, at 9.6 II (iv); note 305, recommendation 4a; E/CN.4/2006; note 274, annex, paras. 12 (a)-(c) and 14 (b).

[297] General Assembly resolution 55/67, para. 17.

[298] See note 120, para. 277.

[299] See note 19, paras. 34, 129 (a), 261, 275, 287; note 23, para. 169 (f); Committee on the Elimination of Discrimination against Women general recommendation 19, article 24 (c); note 15, article 4 (k); note 274, para 13.

[300] Concluding comments issued to 90 States parties between 2001 and 2005 were examined and are reflected in the discussion of the Committee's concerns.

[301] Concluding comments/observations made by the Human Rights Committee, the Committee on Economic, Social and Cultural Rights, the Committee on the Elimination of Racial Discrimination, the Committee on the Rights of the Child and the Committee Against Torture to States parties between 2002 and 2005 were analysed for references to violence against women. During that time, the Committee on Migrant Workers had not yet considered reports of States parties.

[302] International Labour Organization/International Programme on the Elimination of Child Labour (2003) "Good Practices: Gender mainstreaming in actions against child labour", available at: http://www.ilo.org/public/english/standards/ipec/publ/gender/mainstreaming.pdf.

[303] E/CN.4 /2003/75/Add.1, para. 2147.

[304] Unless otherwise stated, the examples in this chapter came from the following sources: Member States' contributions to the Secretary-General's in-depth study on violence against women, available at: http://www.un.org/womenwatch/daw/vaw/responses/index.htm; NGO contributions to the Secretary-General's in-depth study on violence against women, available at: http://www.un.org/womenwatch/daw/vaw/ngo-contributions.htm; responses to the Secretary-General's questionnaire to Governments on Implementation of the Beijing Platform for Action, available at: http://www.un.org/womenwatch/daw/followup/countrylist.htm; responses to the United Nations Secretary-General's Questionnaire to Member States on implementation of the Beijing Platform for Action and the outcome of the twenty-third special session of the General Assembly, available at: http://www.un.org/womenwatch/daw/Review/english/responses.htm; papers prepared for and final report of the Expert Group Meeting "Good practices in combating and eliminating violence against women", organized by the Division for the Advancement of Women in collaboration with the United Nations Office on Drugs and Crime, Vienna, 17-20 May, 2005, available at: http://www.un.org/womenwatch/daw/egm/vaw-gp-2005/index.html; State party reports submitted under article 18 of the Convention on the Elimination of All Forms of Discrimination against Women, available at http://www.un.org/womenwatch/daw/cedaw; UNIFEM, *Not a Minute More, Ending Violence Against Women* (2003) (United Nations publication, Sales No. 05.III.F.2); Council of Europe, *Implementation of and follow-up to Recommendation Rec(2002)5 on the Protection of Women against Violence* (2005), available at: http://www.coe.int/equality; CLADEM, UNIFEM, *Dossier sobre Violencia Domestica en America Latina y el Caribe* (2005); and Rioseco Ortiga, L., *Buenas prácticas para la erradicación de la violencia doméstica en la región de América Latina y el Caribe*, Serie Mujer y Desarrollo No.75, Comision Economica para America Latina y El Caribe (United Nations, Chile, 2005).

[305] See note 1, para. 36.

[306] Ibid., para. 28.

[307] For further information see the following websites: http://www.fundacionmujeres.es; http://www.elmundo.es/; http://www.juntadeandalucia.es/institutodelamujer/; http://www.malostratos.com/; http://www.redfeminista.org.

[308] The Asia Foundation "Combating Violence Against Women" available at: http://www.asiafoundation.org/pdf/violenceagainstwomen.pdf.

[309] See CEDAW/C/PAR/5, p. 19; note 304, Rioseco, 2005, p. 40.

[310] See note 304, Luxembourg response to 10-year review questionnaire.

[311] See CEDAW/C/KOR/5, paras. 95-96.

[312] See note 304, Chile response to 5 year review questionnaire.

[313] See note 304, Netherlands contribution to study.

[314] See note 304, UNIFEM, p. 59.

[315] See note 304, International Association of Women Judges' contribution to study.

[316] See note 304, UNIFEM, 2003, p. 45.

[317] See for example, For a World Free of Violence against Women in Ghana: legal training kit compiled by WiLDAF/FeDDAF Ghana, available at: http://www.wildaf-ao.org/eng/IMG/pdf/soc_ss_violence_Ghana.pdf.

[318] See note 304, Philippines contribution to study.

[319] Combrink, H., *The dark side of the rainbow: violence against women in South Africa after ten years of democracy* (2005) Acta Juridica 174, p. 195; see also South African Police Service National Instruction No. 22/1998 "Sexual offences: Support to victims and crucial aspects of the investigation"; South African Police Service National Instruction (no. 16); National Prosecutors' Directives.

[320] See note 304, United Kingdom and Northern Ireland contribution to study.

[321] See note 304, Nepal contributions to study.

[322] "EWL Observatory", available at: http://www.womenlobby.org.

[323] "National Observatories", available at: http://www.womenlobby.org.

[324] See note 304, CLADEM, UNIFEM.

[325] Introduced as Bill C-49 in 1991, now section 277 of the Criminal Code; note that evaluations of this law have suggested the need for further improvement in implementation and judicial interpretation. See Canadian Department of Justice (1997) "Technical Report: Implementation Review of Bill C-49", available from: http://www.justice.gc.ca/en/ps/rs/rep/1997/tr97-1a.html.

[326] See note 304, CEDAW/C/TUN/3-4, para. 59. Note, however, that this law provides that withdrawal of the case by a victim who is an ascendant or spouse shall terminate any proceedings, trial or enforcement of penalty.

[327] See note 304, Turkey contribution to study.

[328] See note 304, Rioseco, p. 41; note 319, p. 191.

[329] See note 304, Vienna EGM expert paper.

[330] "Family Violence Intervention Program" available at: http://www.dvcs.org.au/Resources/FVIP%20info%20for%20WEBSITE.doc.

[331] CEDAW/C/LKA/3-4, p.14.

[332] E/CN.4/2003/75, para. 37.

[333] See note 304, Finland, Japan, Nepal and the United Kingdom and Northern Ireland responses to 5 year review questionnaire.

[334] See note 304, Vienna EGM final report, p. 18.

[335] See note 304, Egypt response to 5 year review questionnaire.

[336] Information at www.equalitynow.org.

[337] See note 304, Vienna EGM final report, p. 18.

[338] See note 304, Vienna EGM expert paper, Logar, R.

[339] Act to Improve Civil Court Protection against Acts of Violence and Unwelcome Advances as well as to Facilitate the Allocation of the Marital Dwelling in the event of Separation, entered into force 1 January 2002.

[340] E/CN.4/1996/53, para. 126.

[341] See note 329, p. 8.

[342] Ibid.

[343] Ibid, p. 13.

[344] See note 304, Philippines contribution to study

[345] See note 304, United Kingdom and Northern Ireland contribution to study.

[346] See note 304, South Africa contribution to study.

[347] Larrain, S., "Curbing domestic violence: Two decades of action", Inter-American Development Bank, available at: http://idbdocs.iadb.org/wsdocs/getdocument.aspx?docnum=361449.

[348] See note 304, Ibid.

[349] See note 304, Dominican Republic response to 10 year review questionnaire.

[350] "Belgium: Trafficking in human beings", available at: http://www.legislationline.org, Trafficking in Human Beings/Belgium/Analysis.

[351] Schneider, E., *Battered Women and Feminist Lawmaking* (New Haven, Yale University Press, 2000), pp. 148-78, 196-98; and Goldscheid, J., "The Civil Rights Remedy of the 1994 Violence Against Women Act: Struck Down But Not Ruled Out", *Family Law Quarterly*, vol. 39, No. 1 (Spring 2005).

[352] *Carmichele v. Minister of Safety and Security 2001* (10) BCLR 995 (CC).

[353] *Vishaka v. The State of Rajasthan*, 1997 SOL Case No. 177 (Supreme Court of India).

[354] See note 304, Vienna EGM expert paper, Kelly, L., p. 7.

[355] See note 304, Republic of Korea contribution to study.

[356] United States Office to Monitor and Combat Trafficking in Persons, *Trafficking in Persons Report 2004* (Washington D.C., U.S. Department of State, 2004) available at http://www.state.gov/g/tip/rls/tiprpt/2004/33192.htm.

[357] Council of Europe, Group of Specialists for Combating Violence against Women, *Final Report of Activities of the EG-S-VL including a Plan of Action for combating violence against women* (Strasbourg, Council of Europe, 1997), available at: http://www.coe.int/T/E/Human_Rights/Equality/PDF_EG-S-VL(97)1_E.pdf.

[358] Women against Violence Europe, *Away from Violence. European Guidelines for Setting up and Running a Women's Refuge, Manual* (Vienna, Women against Violence Europe, 2004), available at: http://www.wave-network.org/start.asp?b=6&sub=14.

[359] Council of Europe, *Implementation of and Follow-up to Recommendation Rec(2002)5 on the Protection of Women against Violence* (Strasbourg, Council of Europe, 2005), p. 81, available at: http://www.coe.int/equality. All the shelters except one in Dubno, which admits victims of trafficking, admit only victims of domestic violence.

[360] Economic and Social Commission for Asia and the Pacific, *Sexually abused and sexually exploited children and youth in Pakistan: A qualitative assessment of their health needs and available services in selected provinces* (New York, United Nations, 2001), available at: www.unescap.org/esid/hds/sexual/pakistan.pdf.

[361] See note 304, Vienna EGM expert paper, Carcedo, C.

[362] See note 304, Vienna EGM expert paper, Mladjenovic, L.

[363] See note 304, GABRIELA contribution to study.

[364] See note 304, E/CN.4/1997/47, para. 96.

[365] See note 304, Reaching Out Romania contribution to study.

[366] See note 304, Singapore contribution to study.

[367] See note 304, Greece contribution to the study.

[368] See note 39.

[369] See note 304, Australia contribution to study.

[370] See note 304, Denmark contribution to study.

[371] See note 97.

[372] Centre for Women's Global Leadership, "16 Days of Activism against Gender Violence" available online at: http://www.cwgl.rutgers.edu/16days/home.html.

[373] See note 304, Vienna EGM expert paper, Michau, L.

[374] See Michau, L. and Naker, D., *Mobilizing Communities to Prevent Domestic Violence: A Resource Guide for Organizations in East and Southern Africa* (Kampala, Raising Voices, 2003); *Raising Voices, Impact Assessment. Mobilising Communities to Prevent Domestic Violence* (Kampala, Raising Voices, 2003); and Bott, S., Morrison, A. and Ellsberg, M., "Preventing and responding to gender-based violence in middle and low-income countries: a global review and analysis", *World Bank Policy Research Working Paper No. 3618* (Washington D.C., World Bank, 2005), available at: http://ideasrepec.org/p/wbk/wbrups/3618.html.

[375] Abdel-Hadi, A., *We Are Decided: The Struggle of an Egyptian Village to Eradicate Female Circumcision* (Cairo, Cairo Institute for Human Rights, 1997).

[376] See www.whiteribbon.ca.

[377] See note 304, Vienna EGM expert paper, Fisher, H.

[378] See note 304, UNIFEM, p. 29.

[379] Ibid., p. 20; Violence against Women Specialist Unit, "16 Days of Activism a big success in NSW", available at: http://www.lawlink.nsw.gov.au/lawlink/vaw/ll_vaw.nsf/pages/vaw_vaw_iaatrcampaign.

[380] See note 304, UNIFEM, p. 28.

[381] Raising Voices and UN-Habitat's Safer Cities Programme, *Preventing gender-based violence in the Horn, East and Southern Africa*, 2004, available at: http://www.unhabitat.org/programmes/safercities/documents/preventgbv.pdf, pp. 58-59.

[382] These and future recommendations will continuously be made available at the website.

Prevalence of physical assaults on women by a male partner

Country or area	Year of study	Region covered	Sample size	Study population	Age (years)	Proportion of women physically assaulted by a partner — last 12 months	Ever
AFRICA							
Ethiopia	2002	Meskanena Wored[a]	2,261	III	15-49	29	49
Kenya	1984-1987	Kisii District	612	V	>15		42[b]
Malawi[c]	2005	National	3,546				30
Namibia	2003	Windhoek	1,367	III	15-49	16	31
South Africa	1998	Eastern Cape	396	III	18-49	11	27
	1998	Mpumalanga	419	III	18-49	12	28
	1998	Northern Province	464	III	18-49	5	19
	1998	National	10,190	II	15-49	6	13
Uganda	1995-1996	Lira and Masaka	1,660	II	20-44		41[b]
United Republic of Tanzania	2002	Dar es Salaam	1,442	III	15-49	15	33
	2002	Mbeya	1,256	III	15-49	19	47
Zambia	2001-2002	National	3,792	III	15-49	27	49
Zimbabwe	1996	Midlands Province	966	I	>18		17[d]

Country or area	Year of study	Region covered	Sample size	Study population	Age (years)	Proportion of women physically assaulted by a partner — last 12 months	Ever
LATIN AMERICA AND THE CARIBBEAN							
Barbados	1990	National	264	I	20-45		30[e,f]
Brazil	2001	Sao Paulo	940	III	15-49	8	27
	2001	Pernambuco	1,188	III	15-49	13	35
Chile	1993	Santiago Province	1,000	II	22-55		26[b]
	1997	Santiago	310	II	15-49	23	
	2004[9]	Santa Rosa	422	IV	15-49	4	25
Colombia	1995	National	6,097	II	15-49		19[b]
	2000	National	7,602	III	15-49	3	44
Dominican Republic	2002	National	6,807	III	15-49	11	22
Ecuador	1995	National	11,657	II	15-49	12	
El Salvador	2002	National	10,689	III	15-49	6	20[b]
Guatemala	2002	National	6,595	VI	15-49	9	
Honduras	2001	National	6,827	VI	15-49	6	10
Haiti	2000	National	2,347	III	15-49	21	29

LATIN AMERICA AND THE CARIBBEAN (cont'd)

Country or area	Year of study	Region covered	Sample size	Study population	Age (years)	Proportion of women physically assaulted by a partner — last 12 months	Ever
Mexico	1996	Guadalajara	650	III	>15		27
	1996[g]	Monterrey	1,064	III	>15		17
	2003	National	34,184	II	>15	9	
Nicaragua	1995	Leon	360	III	15-49	27	52
	1997	Managua	378	III	15-49	33	69
	1998	National	8,507	III	15-49	13	30
Paraguay	1995-1996	National	5,940	III	15-49		10
	2004	National	5,070	III	15-44	7	19
Peru	2000	National	17,369	III	15-49	2	42
	2001	Lima	1,019	III	15-49	17	50
	2001	Cusco	1,497	III	15-49	25	62
Puerto Rico	1995-1996	National	4,755	III	15-49		13[h]
Uruguay	1997	National	545	II[i]	22-55	10[f]	

Country or area	Year of study	Region covered	Sample size	Study population	Age (years)	Proportion of women physically assaulted by a partner — last 12 months	Ever
NORTH AMERICA							
Canada	1993	National	12,300	I	>18	3 [d,f]	29 [d,f]
	1999	National	8,356	III	>15	3	8 [i]
United States of America	1995-1996	National	8,000	I	>18	1 [e]	22 [e]
ASIA AND WESTERN PACIFIC							
Australia	1996	National	6,300	I		3 [a]	8 [b,d]
	2002-2003	National	6,438	III	18-69	3	31
Bangladesh	1992	National (villages)	1,225	II	<50	19	47
	1993	Two rural regions	10,368	II	15-49		42 [b]
	2003	Dhaka	1,373	III	15-49	19	40
	2003	Matlab	1,329	III	15-49	16	42
Cambodia	1996	Six regions	1,374	III	15-49	16	16
	2000	National	2,403	III	15-49	15	18
China	1999-2000	National	1,665	II	20-64	15	15

ASIA AND WESTERN PACIFIC (cont'd)

Country or area	Year of study	Region covered	Sample size	Study population	Age (years)	Proportion of women physically assaulted by a partner — last 12 months	Ever
India	1998-2000	National	90,303	III	15-49	10	19
	1999	Six states	9,938	III	15-49	14	40
	2004[9]	Lucknow	506	IV	15-49	25	35
	2004[9]	Trivandrum	700	IV	15-49	20	43
	2004[9]	Vellore	716	IV	15-49	16	31
Indonesia	2000	Central Java	765	IV	15-49	2	11
Japan	2001	Yokohama	1,276	III	18-49	3	13
New Zealand	2002	Auckland	1,309	III	18-64	5	30
	2002	North Waikato	1,360	III	18-64		34
Papua New Guinea	2002	National, rural villages	628	III[i]			67
Philippines	1993	National	8,481	IV	15-49		10
	1998	Cagayan de Oro City and Bukidnon	1,660	II	15-49		26
	2004[9]	Paco	1,000	IV	15-49	6	21
Republic of Korea	2004	National	5,916	II	20 -	13.2	20.7

Country or area	Year of study	Region covered	Sample size	Study population	Age (years)	Proportion of women physically assaulted by a partner — last 12 months	Ever
ASIA AND WESTERN PACIFIC (cont'd)							
Samoa	2000	National	1,204	III	15-49	18	41
Tajikistan[k]	2005	Khatlon region	400	I	17-49	19	36
Thailand	2002	Bangkok	1,048	III	15-49	8	23
	2002	Nakonsawan	1,024	III	15-49	13	34
Viet Nam	2004	Ha Tay province	1,090	III	15-60	14	25
EUROPE							
Albania	2002	National	4,049	III	15-44	5	8
Azerbaijan	2001	National	5,533	III	15-44	8	20
Finland	1997	National	4,955	I	18-74		30
France	2002	National	5,908	II	>18	3	9[l]
Georgia	1999	National	5,694	III	15-44	2	5
Germany	2003	National	10,264	III	16-85		23[d]
Lithuania	1999	National	1,010	II	18-74		42[b,d,m]
Netherlands	1986	National	989	I	20-60		21[e]

EUROPE (cont'd)

Country or area	Year of study	Region covered	Sample size	Study population	Age (years)	Proportion of women physically assaulted by a partner — last 12 months	Ever
Norway	1989	Tronheim	111	III	20-49		18
	2003	National	2,143	III	20-56	6	27
Republic of Moldova	1997	National	4,790	III	15-44	8	15
Romania	1999	National	5,322	III	15-44	10	29
Russian Federation	2000	Three provinces	5,482	III	15-44	7	22
Former Serbia and Montenegro	2003	Belgrade	1,189	III	15-49	3	23
Sweden	2000	National	5,868	III	18-64	4[h]	18[h]
Switzerland	1994-1996	National	1,500	II	20-60	6[f]	21[f]
	2003	National	1,882	III	>18		10
Turkey	1998	East and South-East Anatolia	599	I	14-75		58[e]
Ukraine	1999	National	5,596	III	15-44	7	19
United Kingdom of Great Britain and Northern Ireland	1993[g]	North London	430	I	>16	12[e]	30[e]
	2001	National	12,226	I	16-59	3	19[n]

Ending violence against women: From words to action

Country or area	Year of study	Region covered	Sample size	Study population	Age (years)	Proportion of women physically assaulted by a partner — last 12 months	Ever
EASTERN MEDITERRANEAN							
Egypt	1995-1996	National	7,123	III	15-49	13	34
	2004[i]	El-Sheik Zayed	631	IV	15-49	11	11
Israel	1997	Arab population	1,826	II	19-67	32	
West Bank and Gaza Strip	1994	Palestinian population	2,410	II	17-65	52	69

Key
Study population

I: all women

II: currently married/partnered women

III: ever married/partnered women

IV: women with a pregnancy outcome

V: married women—half with pregnancy outcome, half without

VI: women who had a partner within the last 12 months

FOOTNOTES TO ANNEX 1

[a] Source for all countries or areas, unless noted: Ellsberg, M. and Heise, L., *Researching violence against women: a practical guide for researchers and activists* (Washington, D.C., WHO, PATH, 2005).

[b] During current relationship.

[c] Pelser, E. et al. 2005. *Intimate Partner Violence: Results from a National Gender-Based Study in Malawi*, Crime and Justice Statistical Division, National Statistical Office.

[d] Although sample included all women, rate of abuse is shown for ever married/partnered women (number not given).

[e] Sample group included women who had never been in a relationship and therefore were not in exposed group.

[f] Physical or sexual assault.

[g] Publication date (field work dates not reported).

[h] Rate of partner abuse among ever married/partnered women recalculated from author's data.

[i] Non-random sampling methods used.

[j] Within the last five years.

[k] Haar, Robin N., *Violence Against Women in Marriage: A General Population Study in Khatlon Oblast, Tajikistan*, baseline survey conducted by the NGO Social Development Group (2005).

[l] Since the age of 18.

[m] Includes threats.

[n] Since the age of 16.

Ending violence against women: From words to action

Costs of violence against women: selected studies generating a monetary estimate of costs

Author; date of publication; region/country	Costs (calculated for one year)	Data used (including sample sizes)	Costs covered
Leonard and Cox, Distaff Assoc.; 1991; Australia[a]	**1.5 billion Australian dollars**	– Prevalence based on police call-outs – Records of service providing agencies – Survey of service providing agencies to create case study templates to be used when no data exists. Not clear where per unit costs originate.	– Deaths – Absenteeism, loss of productivity – Accommodation, legal, medical, lost income, lost work time – Health care, welfare delivery, accommodation, income, police, courts, victim compensation, interpreters
Blumel; 1993; Australia[b]	**620 million Australian dollars**	– Original survey of 50 women: 10 victims of physical violence and 40 victims of rape or sexual assault.	– Legal, accommodation, courts, emergency services, police, health, counselling, referral, vehicle and personal effects, lost earnings
Mansingh & Ramphal; 1993; Jamaica[c]	**1.1 billion United States dollars**	– Original survey of 640 victims of interpersonal violence at the Kingston Public Hospital	– Direct medical costs
KPMG; 1994; Australia[d]	**4 million Australian dollars for 40 women (17.67 million Australian dollars for the state of Tasmania, but not a representative sample)**	– Original survey, 40 respondents – Survey of community agencies to provide unit costs	– Loss of property, sick leave, bad debts, change of schools, security measures, legal costs pertaining to custody and access – Telephone advice lines, police, shelter, ambulance, crisis support services, referral services, housing services

Author; date of publication; region/country	Costs (calculated for one year)	Data used (including sample sizes)	Costs covered
Snively; 1994; **New Zealand**[e]	**1.2 to 1.4 billion New Zealand dollars**	– Survey of service providing agencies – Typical template of services created – Base scenario: prevalence equal to police call-outs – Five-times base scenario: multiplies base case by 5 – Income foregone scenario: adds lost earnings – Includes family violence with child victims – Government documents – Prior research	– Medical care, drugs, refuge, relocation, legal costs, dental care, lost earnings – Deaths – Justice, social welfare, shelters and crisis agencies, income support, police, courts
Day; 1995; **Canada**[f]	**1.5 billion Canadian dollars**	– Violence Against Women Survey – National statistical agency publications – Government budgets – Provincial health survey – National crime victimization – Other research results	– Medical, dental, lost time at paid and unpaid work, psychiatry, drug and alcohol abuse, shelters, crisis lines, volunteer time, government support services

Author; date of publication; region/country	Costs (calculated for one year)	Data used (including sample sizes)	Costs covered
Greaves et al.; 1995; Canada[g]	**4.2 billion Canadian dollars**	– Violence Against Women Survey: 12,300 sample – Government statistics – Prior research results – Expert opinion	– Lost earnings and unpaid work, accommodation, relocation, self-defence – Deaths – Government's lost tax revenues, courts, incarceration, police, legal aid, victim compensation, medical, shelters, counselling, public awareness, research, volunteer hours
Kerr and McLean; 1996; Canada[h]	**385 million Canadian dollars**	– Violence Against Women Survey – Provincial government ministry budgets – National crime victimization survey	– Police, corrections, compensation, social programmes for victims and perpetrators, mental health, alcohol and drug treatment, shelters – Loss of paid and unpaid work time
Miller et al.; 1996; United States of America[i]	**105 billion United States dollars tangible, 450 billion United States dollars including intangibles (cost for all crime)**	– Federal Bureau of Investigation Uniform Crime Reports – National crime victimization survey – Other nationally representative sample surveys – Prior research	– Property damage and loss, medical care for injuries, insurance, victim services, lost earnings and housework – Pain and suffering and death (covers all crime, not limited to violence or women victims)

Author; date of publication; region/country	Costs (calculated for one year)	Data used (including sample sizes)	Costs covered
Korf et al.; 1997; Netherlands[j]	**1 billion Canadian dollars**	– Female victims of domestic violence	– Police and justice, medical, psychosocial care, labour, social security
Stanko et al.; 1998; Hackney, Greater London, United Kingdom of Great Britain and Northern Ireland[k]	**7.5 million British pounds for Hackney, 278 million British pounds for Greater London**	– Original survey of 107 service providers – 26 case studies, composites – Prevalence found from trawling key agency files to find the percentage of caseload resulting from violence – Original survey of 129 women in a doctor's office waiting room. – Results from other research	– Police, courts, legal costs, divorce, public-sector housing, shelter, social workers, physicians, emergency ward, health office
Faley et al.; 1999; United States of America—United States Army[l]	**250 million United States dollars (least cost, 1994 dollars)**	– Examines sexual harassment only – Original survey, 2,079 respondents including males and females – United States Army budgetary documents	– Costs of sexual harassment: Productivity loss, absenteeism, separation, replacement, transfer and other
Godenzi and Yodanis; 1999; Switzerland[m]	**60 million euro**	– Various surveys	– Medical care, police and justice, support, shelters and counselling, State costs, victim-related support, research

Author; date of publication; region/country	Costs (calculated for one year)	Data used (including sample sizes)	Costs covered
Morrison and Orlando; 1999; Chile and Nicaragua[n]	**In Chile: reduced earnings of 1.56 billion United States dollars** **In Nicaragua: reduced earnings of 29.5 million United States dollars**	– Original surveys of 310 and 378 women, respectively	– Employment, health services, children's educational achievement
Henderson and Associates; 2000; Australia[o]	**1.5 billion Australian dollars**	– Examines business sector only – Extrapolations from relevant Australian and international research findings – Consultations with relevant organizations and individuals – Prior research findings	– Business sector costs: absenteeism, turnover, lost productivity – Other costs: tax share of relevant government services, foregone profits from lost income and changes in expenditure patterns of victims, perpetrators and others.

Author; date of publication; region/country	Costs (calculated for one year)	Data used (including sample sizes)	Costs covered
Heiskanen and Piipsa; 2001; Finland[p]	**50 million euro in direct costs** **56 million euro in indirect costs**	– Refers to survey of 7,000 women undertaken for earlier study "Faith, Hope and Battering" by same authors. – Prior research findings of other authors – Statistics from government databases and agency budgets, activity reports, etc. – Interviews with experts to obtain percentage of service use attributable to violence against women – Includes two case studies	– Health including physician visits, hospital care and medication – Shelters, crisis services, social work, therapy, police, trial, prison – Deaths, using human capital approach
Deloitte and Touche, Almenara Estudios Economicos y Sociales; 2002; Andalucía, Spain[q]	**2.4 billion euro**	– 300 women who left their partners and stayed in State-provided shelters	– Includes: social, health, judicial and police sectors, human and emotional costs, employment/economic output – Includes intangibles
Health Canada; 2002; Canada[r]	**1.5 billion Canadian dollars**	– Police: reported and homicide data – 1999 General Social Survey and other data sources	– Direct medical costs

Author; date of publication; region/country	Costs (calculated for one year)	Data used (including sample sizes)	Costs covered
National Center for Injury Prevention and Control; 2003; United States of America[s]	**5.8 billion United States dollars**	– National Violence Against Women Survey, sample size 8,000 (only women who were injured were considered) – Medical Expenditure Panel—Survey – Medicare file	– Medical costs from injuries only – Lost time at paid and unpaid work – Deaths
Bowlus et al.; 2003; Canada[t]	**15.7 billion Canadian dollars (measuring the costs of child abuse in children and adult survivors)**	– Provincial health survey – Government statistics and agency reports – Previous research	– Very comprehensive listing of police, legal, penal, probation, victim compensation, special education, health, social services, lost earnings, and personal costs

Author; date of publication; region/country	Costs (calculated for one year)	Data used (including sample sizes)	Costs covered
Access Economics; 2004; Australia[U]	**8.1 billion Australian dollars**	- Women's Safety Survey - Australian longitudinal study on Women's Health (created a profile of conditions associated with domestic violence since data didn't have victims separated out) - Results from prior research	- Includes all domestic violence regardless of the sex of the victim or perpetrator - Includes pain and suffering, death, and costs of children witnessing adult violence - Government: health, justice, education, community services, accommodation - Personal: property replacement and bad debts, lost time at paid and unpaid work - Business costs of lost productivity, search and hiring, etc. - Includes lost economies of scale in households
Walby; 2004; United Kingdom of Great Britain and Northern Ireland[V]	**5.8 billion British pounds direct and indirect costs, 23 billion British pounds including pain and suffering**	- National Crime Survey including intimate partner violence (BCS IPV): 40,000 sample - Department of Transport reports on accidents and injuries - Service-providing agency reports - Prior research findings	- Very comprehensive listing of criminal justice, health, social services, housing, and civil legal costs - Loss of productivity and earnings to employers and employees - Pain and suffering

FOOTNOTES TO ANNEX 2

[a] Leonard, H. and Cox, E., *Costs of Domestic Violence* (Haymarket, New South Wales Women's Co-ordination Unit, 1991).

[b] Blumel, D. K., Gibb, G. L , Innis, B. N., Justo, D. L. and Wilson, D. W , *Who Pays? The economic costs of violence against women* (Sunshine Coast, Sunshine Coast Interagency Research Group Queensland for the Women's Policy Unit, 1993).

[c] Mansingh A. and Ramphal P., "The nature of interpersonal violence in Jamaica and its strain on the National Health System", *West Indian Medicine Journal*, vol. 42 (1993), pp. 53-56.

[d] KPMG, *Economic Costs of Domestic Violence in Tasmania*, Tasmanian Domestic Violence Advisory Committee (Hobart, Office of the Status of Women, 1994).

[e] Snively, S., The New Zealand Economic Costs of Family Violence (Auckland, Coopers and Lybrand, 1994).

[f] Day, T., *The Health Related Costs of Violence Against Women in Canada: The Tip of the Iceberg* (London, Ontario, Centre for Research on Violence Against Women and Children, 1995).

[g] Greaves, L., Hankivsky, O. and Kingston-Riechers, J., *Selected estimates of the costs of violence against women* (London, Ontario, Centre for Research on Violence Against Women and Children, 1995).

[h] Kerr, R. and McLean, J., *Paying for Violence: Some of the Costs of Violence Against Women in BC* (British Colombia, Ministry of Women's Equality, 1996).

[i] Miller T. R., Cohen, M. A. and Wiersema, B., *Victim Costs and Consequences: A New Look* (U.S. Department of Justice, Office of Justice Programs, National Institute of Justice, 1996).

[j] Korf, D. J., Meulenbeek, H., Mot, E. and van den Brandt, T., *Economic Costs of Domestic Violence Against Women* (Utrecht, Dutch Foundation of Women's Shelters, 1997).

[k] Stanko, E., Crisp, D., Hale, C. and Lucraft, H., *Counting the Costs: Estimating the Impact of Domestic Violence in the London Borough of Hackney* (Swindon, Crime Concern, 1998).

[l] Faley, R. H., Knapp, D. E., Kustis, G. A. and Dubois, C., "Estimating the Organization costs of Sexual Harassment: The Case of U.S. Army", *Journal of Business and Psychology,* vol. 13 (1999), pp. 461-484.

[m] Godenzi, A. and Yodanis, C., *Report on the Economic Costs of Domestic Violence Against Women* (Fribourg, University of Fribourg, Switzerland, 1999).

[n] Morrison, A. R. and Orlando, M. B., 1999, supra note 213.

[o] Henderson, M., *Impacts and Costs of Domestic Violence on the Australian Business/Corporate Sector* (Brisbane, Lord Mayor's Women's Advisory Committee, Brisbane City Council, 2000).

[p] Heiskanen, Markku and Minna Piispa, *The price of Violence: The costs of Men's Violence Against Women in Finland* (Statistic Finland and the Council for Equality, 2001).

[q] Institute for Women of Andalusia, *The Economic and Social Costs of Domestic Violence in Andalusia* (Andalusia, Spain: Institute for Women of Andalusia, 2003).

[r] Health Canada (2002). *Violence against women. Impact of violence on women's health,* available at: http://www.hc-sc.gc.ca.

[s] National Center for Injury Prevention and Control, *Costs of Intimate Partner Violence Against Women in the United States* (Atlanta BA, USA: Centers for Disease Control and Prevention, 2003).

[t] Bowlus, Audra, Katherine McKenna, Tanis Day, and David Wright, *The Economic Costs and Consequences of Child Abuse* (Ottawa, Law Commission of Canada, 2003).

[u] Access Economics, Ltd., *The Cost of Domestic Violence to the Australian Economy, Part I and II* (Office of the Status of Women, Government of Australia, 2004).

[v] Walby, Sylvia, *The Cost of Domestic Violence* (London: Department of Trade and Industry, 2004).

Ending violence against women: From words to action